The Making of a DREAM GIRL

How I Sold and Made MILLIONS in Real Estate

Claudine L. Ellis

DEDICATION

In Loving Memory

Aaron Legum. Thank you for being my business partner and for contributing to my career. I am successful in part because of you. I miss you. I will always love you.

This book is dedicated to the real estate industry for choosing Me. I believe that real estate is the best thing that ever happened to me. I also dedicate this book to each and every client who chose and trusted me, and those individuals who taught me in any capacity, namely-Ann Palmateer who taught me the vast majority of my continuing education classes!

This book is also dedicated to my family: my parents who made sure we grew up in a home, my husband for all his support, and my lovely children who are my WHY.

I especially want to dedicate this book to those who DID NOT help me in any way. It is because of you that I was determined to win.

Thank You!

ACKNOWLEDGMENTS

Well-deserved thanks to my mentor, John Burley--a person who I admire for his business acumen, savvy investment strategies, and phenomenal hands-on training and books. If you ever attend his bootcamps, you'll agree that he is one outstanding, successful investor and person. Mr. Burley creates a working seminar where participants make deals before finishing the class. John, without knowing it, encouraged me to invest and still encourages me. He is very accessible and whenever I'm in Phoenix he takes the time to meet with me. Each time meet or speak with John, I walk away with invaluable business nuggets. Everyone should have a "John" in their corner.

FOREWORD
By John R. Burley

Claudine Ellis has been in the Real Estate Industry for over 15 years, as a top producer, she is very qualified in this area. What I love about this book is that she brings a unique perspective that is desperately needed for the reader.

She is looked upon as a changing face in real estate and once you have read this book, you will definitely have made a paradigm shift. This book highlights new insights and a new voice as a representative of the changing face of the real estate industry.

You will learn to see "best business practices" from a real estate agent who has learned that you need to run it like a business and not just be a real estate agent. This book is geared towards all agents. The new agents seeking to start a career in real estate to the seasoned veteran who need to refocus their businesses and those who are planning for retirement.

It really is key for successful agents who have not planned for their financial future to begin looking at an exit plan. Congratulations if you're a successful agent now! However, it's critical to think long-term in the event that things change, and your commission check stops. It's time for real estate agents to stop thinking like traditional salespeople, but instead, start identifying themselves as "true" businessowners and act accordingly.

In a landscape in which traditional farming methods are still advertised and widely promoted, Claudine emphasizes the possibilities of social media, detailing the way she has leveraged it, to an audience that all too often "sees it" as something of a mystery.

The book debunks many of the myths about real estate. Further Mrs. Ellis makes the book engaging and an easy read by adding ad libs, humor, honesty, facts from her vast and varied experiences throughout her career. Claudine is an amazing lady whom I am proud to have shared with and consider a good friend. I really enjoyed the book and highly recommend it as a "must put in your library". I am most honored that she regards me as her real estate mentor.

John R. Burley, Founder & CEO
Burley & Associates
Investor

CONTENT

INTRODUCTION
There's enough sun to tan us all – So, here's all the shade!

Everyone wants to be a Real Estate Agent. Guess what, pretty much every single person breathing with a high school diploma can become a real estate agent. I love it! Equal opportunity for all. There's no discrimination there. Anyone who knows me knows that I'm all about uplifting and helping others, so if you've got a brain, can pass the test, then *Voila!* You too can become a real estate agent. I digress...Let's stop and think for just a moment, a home is probably one of the biggest, if not THE biggest, purchase of most people's lives. After pondering this, it could seem just a bit scary thinking that a very inexperienced person in business, and in life, could actually be handling legal documents and representing clients in real estate transactions. Come on, don't be so skeptical. Inexperienced, untrained, green, licensed real estate agents are people too. Right???

I have no idea who's going to read this book, but Lord knows I'm about to put this whole disclaimer in here so that I don't have to defend myself later. I suffer from a rare form of *lackoffilteritis* which occurs in many people, but there's absolutely no cure. I do, however, believe in the power of prayer, so there may be hope, but so far, we've been unable to find a cure. When God made me, he forgot a few things, one was a filter. I would take full responsibility for it, but I didn't make myself, therefore, if you have any issues or concerns, PULEEZE take it to God, just like you'd complain to a supervisor if you got strange customer service or if your order didn't get delivered from Amazon.

Each of us are from different places, we've been through different life experiences, and we have our own thoughts and ideas. I KNOW without a shadow of a doubt that each person will have an opinion or two about any and everything, including stuff I put in this book. Take for example, there are so many sweet peaches in Atlanta, if you pick the sweetest of them all and give the same sweet peach to fifteen different people, there will be a few that will say, either they don't like peaches, or that the peach isn't sweet. I say all that to say, you can't please everyone. I'll never aim to please the world. The simple fact is, it's my book, so I can write whatever I want (tongue out) Lol! The most rewarding discovery for me at this very moment is that I'm at an age where I don't let anyone's opinion affect me. When you stop worrying about other imperfect people's opinions about your imperfect life, there's a sense of freedom and peace that'll change your world. Try it and let me know. If you don't get anything else out of this book, I hope that was the one bit of information that will change your life!

This book may shake up a few folks because it's all ME, raw and right to the point. I hold nothing back. I don't have to. People spend a lot of time being fake, leaving out the *real* information and do all this *speaking in circles* stuff. *Ain't nobody got time for that.* You buy a book or go to a class or seminar and all you leave with is a great feeling. I have no interest in feelings. I wanna know what to do, how to do it, and can you help ME do it. If you did it, then what will it take to help me get there? Other than that, I don't like hearing about all the other *noise*, as I call it. It just makes me anxious. I'm known for telling it exactly the way it should be told. Who has time for games and fluff anyway? I sure don't, and I'm hoping you're trying to be booked and busy so you won't have time to be fooling around with useless materials, conferences, and events that don't immediately change the way you do business or help you get into production. I think people are sometimes scared to share, because they're worried that someone is going to outdo them or take their place. Wow! The entitlement, the jealousy, the foolishness. Don't people know that what is for you is for YOU? I can't understand people sometimes, but that's the world we live in. The truth about what makes most people successful should be shared.

I'm about to give you the good, the bad, and the outright truth! Oh, there's some ugly too. You know I *keeps it 100%*. If you ain't ready, then close the book now! It's about to get real! Let me not forget to also warn that there's a few *Claudine-isms* throughout this read, along with a LOT of slang and broken English, some of which you may have already caught by now, but that's how I roll. You'll be able to follow just fine, but if you can't, just grab a millennial for translation purposes or just follow Cardi B, "Okuuuurrr!" My two favorite Claudine-isms, the ones I'm known for are, *"Lawd!"* and, *"Oh Gawd!"* Buckle up, here I come...*Lawd* (See)!

The conventional, traditional, way of thinking is for

9

the average person. As a result, there comes this shock wave that goes through one's body when they hear a viewpoint that differs from their good old cliché-type, ingrained, old-school mentality. Don't fret, once the shock wears off and you open your mind, you'll get it. Otherwise, you'll just be where you were before we met on this page. *Heehee.*

Unicorn thinkers are not like the average thinkers of course. We don't think about a cup being half full or half empty, instead we think about manufacturing the cup. I certainly don't like the common phrase, "Think outside the box." Uh, I'm a unicorn, so there's no box to begin with. *Ya think?* The proverbial box was designed for the average thinker anyway, so, for me, that was a weird phrase from the outset.

Here's what I learned a long time ago which helped me understand me in the world of others. Given that we're all different, living among different thinkers in the world, I had to realize exactly who I was in a world of different thinkers. Foolish me thought everyone thought like I did or should! My type of thinker is frustrated half the time with those who don't get it. Whatever *it* is. For example, I could be saying something that I think is very rudimentary or in my mind, it's simple and easy to grasp, yet another person doesn't get it as clear as I get it. Nothing is wrong with that, but I used to look all perplexed, trying to make sense of it, but now, I realize that we all don't get it at the same time. It can take longer for some of us, and unfortunately, some of us never get it. No different than when an engineer tries to explain C++ language to me, I'm looking like a deer in headlights!

Engineers get it, but they can't expect me to get it because I'll never get C++ language until I get some training. I know that's more of a technical analogy, but I had to drive the point home.

The *it* that I was talking about was more like trying to get people out of their ironclad way of thinking. For example, when I try to educate folks on how to invest, showing them real simple breakdowns of how they can secure their future, they just don't get it. It's very frustrating. My frustration comes from the fact that I'm trying too hard to help and the person who needs the help isn't receiving it, therefore, they remain unhelped. Anyone who considers themselves solutions-based would be eaten up inside if they had to walk away from a problem without a satisfactory solution. My former transaction coordinator used to joke me by mentioning that I used more brain cells than anyone she knew! That's so far from the truth! The difference between me and others is that I refuse to leave a problem without a solution in any situation, work or life. Lots of people give up or don't investigate, they listen to what others tell them or they just don't care.

There are approximately two million licensed real estate agents working at any one time in the United States, yet each year upwards of ninety five percent of new agents leave the industry. Why? The number one reason cited, an inability to make a living as a real estate agent. *But wait, how is that possible? I thought real estate was easy. If it were easy, then why the mass exodus?* Even those agents with a client base are often insolvent because of an inability to manage money, or to cost-effectively market themselves and/or their business. Did you know that a fair amount of real estate agents don't even own one single home? A lot of real estate agents are operating on a hope and a prayer. *Ooooohh, that's not good.* This makes no sense. Can you imagine this as a career, much less your lifestyle? If this information was presented to you at the outset, would you consider real estate? Many wouldn't, but I would. That's because I don't let anything deter me, I will defy odds, and if anyone can succeed, then I should be able to succeed too. When you have a winning mentality, then nothing is too challenging. I think it's important to look at the positive. There's that cliché of half full, half empty again that people box themselves into. We can certainly use that scenario. We can say that half full is good and half empty is bad. So, if you know that some fail and some succeed, then which half do you want to be in? That's how I think. I know for sure I want to be in the half full group, so there's nothing that will stop me. When folks tell you about other people's failures, they're giving you warning signs that you too can fail. *Uh, this is where the Unicorn in me comes in. EX-CUU-SE (neck roll) Me! See, I'm not them. How dare you put me in their category?* I loathe being compared to failures, but of course the person telling me that doesn't know it. Then this is when it gets real cute, *(don't forget, I suffer from a rare form of lackoffilteritis)* when I tell the person about how I feel, they end up mad at me because they thought I had too much nerve checking them for putting me in a category for which I clearly didn't belong. Whew! They were not ready. *Lawd!*

Some agents find themselves working long after they would prefer to retire because of a lack of financial planning during their careers. Real estate agents are no different from other professionals, it's just how it is. We all have these big retirement dreams, but we don't plan properly, then we wake up at 65 and wonder why. With no retirement savings set aside, many professionals find themselves working well into their 70s, and beyond, in order to generate a livable income.

My hope is that real estate agents will stop living from deal to deal, check to check, without carefully planning for their financial future as a whole. For many real estate practitioners, that last deal is their last dollar. Sounds shocking to some, but I know it to be true because I've seen it. I'm always shocked when I'm spending money with one of my agent buddies and they're a little *short* on funds. I'm scratching my head, thinking, "You guys make a whole lot of money, so why don't you have money for this trip?" Truth is, many really don't have savings. Some are really holding on by a thread. The way real estate works, you don't get paid until the deal closes. You can taste, smell, almost touch that closing check, but until it closes, you're living with hope and desperation. There are times when the money has been accounted for or spent and the deal doesn't go through. In these economic times, it's important that agents take a hard look at how they're doing business. In the blink of an eye, the industry could change and many will be left by the wayside. My suggestion is that agents start thinking bigger and bigger. The time is now! You know what they say, "There's no time like the present."

This seems like as good a time as any to make yet another disclaimer before we jump in any further. Sometimes, reinforcement is needed therefore, I just feel the need. You know I only do this stuff because I want to be sure to let you know that before you read one more thing, this is an unorthodox way of learning. With anything new or different from what you've been preconditioned to, you must retrain the mind. If your mind is closed and not ready for expansion, then you may want to stop right here so we don't have any problems. Everything begins with mindset! If you change your mind, you change your world. So please open your mind!

Let's get right into it. This isn't the type of book that's gonna waste your time. It's common sense stuff and stuff you already know, but never really took time to realize that you knew. Now I'm the voice of what everyone is thinking, but nobody is saying. Lol! As it relates to real estate, most, if not all of you, have been doing this thing backwards for years! Including me when I first started! I didn't know better and there was nobody, and I mean not a single soul there to tell me. Now that I know better, I'm going to do better and I'm telling all of you. So buckle up and enjoy the ride, that's if you're ready!

CHAPTER 1

What is a Dream Girl?
Or Should we ask Who......?

I'm your Dream Girl! I AM REAL ESTATE! I love real estate. Real estate has been the most rewarding career for me. It's an extension of who I am. I can't see myself doing anything but real estate. There's nothing in the world that I would want to do other than real estate. When someone asks me what I do for fun, my response is, "Real estate!" I don't turn it off. Why? When you love it, it's not work. I can't get enough of it! I wake up thinking about it and I fall asleep with it on my mind. I love it, breathe it, and sleep it. We're inseparable. My Facebook profile says, "I am Real Estate." I consider real estate an extension of who I am. If someone said I couldn't do real estate anymore, it would be equivalent to someone telling a singer that he/she couldn't sing anymore. For any passionate singer, that would be the worst news ever! Singing is life, and without her voice, she would feel like it's over! As for me, if I can't do real estate, then it's over for me too. Just put a fork in me because I wouldn't be able to function. I'm so thankful to the shelter industry for giving me the privilege to work as a real estate professional. It's truly an honor.

A Dream Girl is Extremely Passionate

Real estate is my passion. There's nothing in the world that I'd want to do other than real estate. If people are talking to me and it's not about real estate, I'm not fully tuned in. I'm always, always, thinking about my clients, my transactions, where I'm getting my next deal, and how many new clients, pendings, and listings I have. When I visit another state or country, I can't leave without looking at properties. I get my high from real estate. When my phone rings, no matter if it's 2:00 a.m., if it's a potential client who wants my services, I'm over the moon! I'm as excited now about every transaction as if it were my very first. I just love real estate and everything about it. I'm all things real estate. Real estate gives me freedom, convenience, great lifestyle choices, and so much more. When you find something that you love to do, then marry that with the fact that it pays you well, you're living the dream. I'm your Dream Girl!

About once a week I hear this from folks who don't know me and whom I've never met: "Girl you need to slow down! When do you sleep? All you do is real estate, don't you have a hobby? When do you have time for yourself?" The people that feel that way have jobs that they don't love; they're definitely broke, and very unhappy. I take four vacations a year, yet these same folks asking me to slow down don't take any vacations, much less leave their driveway. I work for myself and I make as much money as I want to hustle for, which affords me whatever I want. There are no limits. It baffles me to think that a broke person with a J.O.B. (which means Just Over Broke) would think I need advice about what I do. A lot of people I know with good paying jobs are disgruntled and complain constantly. They stay in their unfulfilling positions because of the salary. A salary is just a bribe to help stifle your dreams so that you can build someone else's dream. It's a systematic institution that we've bought into. If you're great at what you do, then why not work hard for yourself instead of someone else?

A Dream Girl is a Machine

I don't slow down because I'm a machine. Real estate is a 25 hours, eight days a week lifestyle for me. I usually tell people that I'm not a workaholic, I'm a loveaholic. When you love what you do, it's not work, it's fun! If you've ever been in love, you can remember how much you wanted to see your boo. You couldn't stand to be without him or her. Same with me and real estate! I love it and can't live without it. I can't stop and won't stop. I'm not in it for the fortune or fame, but the love of the game. No one works harder and smarter. I don't stop when I'm tired, I stop when I'm done. Sleep is not an option when work is unfinished. Sleep is the new broke. I get the sleep I need when I need it. My body tells me when to take a break. I'm conditioned to do what I do. It takes practice, dedication, and discipline. I'm made for this. I'm no stranger to hard work. I don't need a hobby
other than real estate. I've got the best hobby in the world, I get to meet fabulous people and look at gorgeous homes all

day. What more can I ask for? The best part of my life is that I can do my hobby and get paid extremely well for it.

A Dream Girl is a Hustler

People can't understand my passion and are overwhelmed by my hustle. The level of your income is determined by the level of your hustle. I'm a real estate Olympian. I'm in a contact sport. I'm hungry, always ready, constantly grinding. Call me Jordan. I shoot 1,000 free throws a day. I'm calling, doing lead generation, reading daily to hone my craft. I'm on the field of play, meeting folks, networking, and putting my name out there. Passion goes a long way. When you're genuinely passionate, it shows. My passion wakes me up in the morning, not an alarm clock. If people don't get you, that's ok, then they're not your tribe. You probably just need new people. It's not about others. It's about you. Opinions don't make deposits. I don't believe in failure. I'm destined to be great and to do great things. I realize that integrity is a very important trait. I'm the quick thinking, fast learning, won't let anyone see me sweat type. I can take anything, but I'm also sensitive at times. For the most part, I never give humans power over me. I'm in complete control of me. I don't drink, not even socially, I don't smoke or curse for the most part. *I am practicing my cursing because I want to give it to someone really good, I mean good.* I don't use foul language in front of the kids or clients. I don't like filthy talking females, so I don't want to be one. I have to respect you, for you to affect me. I never let people get inside my head. Life is to be lived and I live it daily. I do what I want, how I want it, and I sing when people are looking. I happen to say my thoughts out loud. I'm me and that's my power.

What separates me from some of my counterparts is that I never say NO! That's my choice. I work harder and smarter than anyone I know. I will work until I meet the goals I set for myself. Did you hear that? Not the goals that YOU or anyone set for me, but the goals I set for myself. The main problem I see with people these days is that they don't know their WHY. If you know your WHY, then you don't need to worry about how to measure success. You would not measure success based on how others are doing. If you want a Ford and someone wants a Bugatti then fine. It's YOUR goal. I dream big. I want more. I can't get enough. I don't let others dictate what's best for me. Only I know what's best for me. Only I know what I want. There are different phases of life and in each phase, there are different needs, and as a result, goals may change. I'm the only one who can decide when, where, or how my goals change or evolve. I always tell people that I'm no smarter than anyone else. The difference between me and the next person is that I have a vision and believe that I can do it. There is nothing that can stop me. If I say I'm going to the moon, please check out the local news, because I'll be strapped up and on my way to the moon, baby! I don't let anything stop me. And guess what, you don't have to let anything stop you! All you have to do is believe!

I say this all the time but very few people get it. Success is not hard because each and every person has the same 25 hours and 8 days a week. Your success is right in front of you. All you need is consistency, discipline and integrity. You have to have a burning desire to win each and every day like your life depends on it. .

If you were to become a Dream Girl or Dream Boy, which is a quintessential Dream Agent, you would know that a Dream Girl believes in being excellent in all areas of life. Some people are destined to succeed but a Dream Girl is determined to succeed. Dream Girls do what they say when they say. Integrity is a key trait of a Dream Girl. Failure is NOT an option for a Dream Girl. A Dream Girl's mission, vision, and goal is to ensure each and every client has the most outstanding experience ever!

This, my friends, is a Dream Girl!

CHAPTER 2

Who are you?
What is a Real Estate Agent?

Perhaps I should start with what a real estate agent is NOT! An agent doesn't just look cute or handsome and run around town showing properties to nice people. Agents don't make, as some would say, "All this money, but do very little work." The money in real estate is not easy money as many would say. If it were easy, we'd all be doing it.

The job title may be that of, real estate agent, but your real job function is that of a problem solver. I say just call yourself a problem solver, point blank, period. That's it. Everything in real estate is a problem, starting with the transaction, the other agent, the house, the inspection report, the title, the buyer, the seller, and oh yes, you. I really want you to change your thought pattern for just a moment. Don't think of the word *problem* in a negative way. I know the first thing you envisioned when you read the word problem was something negative. Let's go back to grade school. When you were in third grade the teacher may have said, "Pull out your math books class, today we're going to work on our math problems, pages six through nine, problems A through F."

We all worked on our problems now didn't we? *I'm not even going to speak under my breath about some of y'all who didn't care to do any schoolwork but we're not going to go there. I have a book to finish writing. Lawd.* Let's compare real estate to third grade math problems, and you're the problem solver. As the problem solver, your job is to find a solution to the problem. It's like solving for X. There's no right answer sometimes. You just have to get to the closing table. Problem solvers are solution-based individuals. They're calm, cool, and collected because their only function, is to solve the problem. The reason why I've lasted in this business so long is because I enter every transaction knowing that I have to first identify the problem, or problems, and then go after the solutions, this mentality makes my job so much easier. If every transaction was problem free, then this would be the job that everyone would want. I don't think there's really any job that's problem free. Real estate has a lot of unknowns. You're always solving for X. At a moment's notice, out of the blue, a curve ball can come your way. If you're a negative person, you will not be invested in finding a solution because you'd rather find someone to blame for the problem.

One of the main issues I see in real estate is that there are many real estate agents who don't know what their job title really is. If they knew what their job was, and that is one of a problem solver, then they'd focus more time and attention on solving the problem. Instead, some are fighting during a transaction, getting mad, fussing folks out, and making things so difficult, it makes the industry so unpleasant at times. When I train new agents, I warn them that when an agent on the other side of a transaction is acting unprofessional, stupid, or crazy, it's not usually about the transaction. Those ornery agents are unhappy in their personal lives and lots of them are broke. The ones who exhibit unprofessional behavior but are not broke, are usually just cocky prima donnas. You know the type, mad when things don't go their way. I'm a winner, so I'm gonna win. If anyone comes up against me with foolishness, they better get some Percocet and a therapist because they're gonna be big mad for a minute. I never lose. I mean never. I don't play to lose. The reason I don't lose is because if I don't get what I want, then I can move on. They lose. It's like a good game of chess. If you can't play chess, then I can't help you. This real estate game is not for everyone.

Real estate for me is like second nature. It comes very natural to me which means that when people see me actively working in real estate, they tend to think it's easy. It's all about systems. Any system that runs smoothly looks easy. Did you ever notice that? For years, I've taken clients out on the first day I met them and they bought a home. My cohorts tell me that they can't seem to do this. I don't get it. I know unequivocally if I find the client exactly what he/she wants, then there's no reason why they wouldn't buy. The only reason why they wouldn't buy is if they're not real buyers. Some are not serious about buying and that's not my fault. A few people doubted me or thought that I was kidding when I said my clients bought homes on the first visit and usually the first house they saw, so I started taking new agents along to prove a point. I had to show them that it wasn't magic. The trick was, there was no trick! It was the system. My system is set up so that there are processes that happen prior to meeting the client that allow them to make the final decision once we meet face to face. My system is so tight, I can sell a home to someone who's never met me or seen the house in person. I've sold homes for sellers whom I've never met and moreover, I've never even seen their home. Systems people, systems. It's amazing. My best deal was when I was in Dubai and my client from San Diego wanted to buy a home out of state. I got it done. Gotta say I'm proud of myself for making these things happen. It's like riding a bike. You don't really know how to do it at first, but the second time, you're riding like a champ. I'm a real estate Olympian at this point. *KeeKee!* I've had the pleasure of training and coaching with many other agents on how to do these simple, yet effective techniques and it's changed their lives.

I also equate being a real estate agent to being a caregiver. Your job is to take care of your clients' needs at the highest level. I share with my coaching students that the best way to stay out of trouble in real estate is to treat your clients like your family members. Of course the ones you love. *Cuz I know some of y'all got some crazy family members that you don't want nothing to do with. Lawd!* When I meet a client, I size them up by age. For example, if they're my kid's age then I consider them my child. If they're my grandma's age then I would think of them as I would my grandma. During the entire transaction, would you honestly say that you treated that client like you would want your son or grandma to be treated? If the answer is no, then you've messed up. I see a lot of issues in real estate and I wonder if that person would like it if their parent, child, or close friend were treated unfairly. The problem is that when an agent is desperate for that check, they sometimes allow the money to cloud their better judgement. Once again, take my advice and remember that the only way I believe you'll never ever go wrong, is if you treat each and every client as your own. Just take care of your client the way you would want to be taken care of.

Real estate agents have the potential to make a lot of money, depending on how hard they hustle. Your hustle determines your income, but that's true for any business. I don't recommend anyone get into real estate because of the money. Don't chase the dollar. If you chase the passion, the money will come.

If you decide to become a real estate agent and you belong to the National Association of Realtors, you then earn the designation of REALTOR®. Not all real estate agents are REALTORS®. It's a choice and some elect not to become a REALTOR®. If you're blessed to become a REALTOR®, please and I mean please, learn how to say the word. There's only one pronunciation for the word REALTOR®. Some people tend to think that REALTOR® is pronounced Real-uh-ter, Real-i-ter, Real-a-ter, Re-AL-i-ter and a few more variations. *I'm actually getting mad just typing it.* The public may not know how it should be pronounced, but by God if you're a real estate agent who's a REALTOR® then you have absolutely no excuse for not knowing how to say your own profession correctly! I've heard every excuse known to man as to why it's pronounced incorrectly. Here are a few: "Everybody says it that way! It's because of where I'm from. It's my dialect. Who cares, as long as I know what it is?"

Here's my comeback phrase (meanwhile they're still pronouncing it incorrectly). So if you go to a doctor and he refers to himself as a Doc-uh-ter, will you be ok with that? Then it makes them think. I'm so annoyed at how many in the industry mispronounce REALTOR®. *I think I should stop right here because now my skin is boiling.* It's my biggest pet peeve to think that a person in a career of mine doesn't even care about the way they pronounce their hard-earned title! I think of all the sleepless nights, the days of studying, and how hard the test was. I wear this badge called REALTOR® with honor and what I won't do is allow anyone to mispronounce the name. I wear it proudly! If I could revoke the license of anyone who can't say their own profession correctly, then I would, but I'm not President, yet. Look out cuz that may just happen. *Lol! Y'all do NOT want me to be President. Nobody would be ready.*

Finally, know what your job is, take care of your clients, and for goodness sake, please know how to pronounce your profession!

CHAPTER 3

You are NOT ready!
The 'REAL' truth about Real Estate School

Real estate school is just that. It's a school where you take a course and are taught how to pass a test. Please don't think that you're going to become the best real estate agent in the world after you take the real estate exam. You're not actually learning everyday real estate practices in a real estate class. You're only learning how to pass the test so you can get your license. If I had to take the test right now, I would probably fail it. Just to make it sound even worse, I actually teach the real estate class! The test is ridiculous! It's confusing, tricky, and full of terms I may never use or see the minute I step outside the classroom. I'm told that the reason for the test is to test one's reasoning and problem-solving skills. All it did was test my patience and got on my nerves. I passed it the very first try because failure is not an option for me. They were not getting my $80 retake fee again. Oh, heck no! I personally know at least ten people who failed it five times or more. Listen, I got too much pride, so if I ever failed it, I would never tell a soul but God. I see people bragging about how they failed the test 21 times and they make over six figures. I wanna dive through the computer and tell them to shut up goofy, no one cares! You passed, let it go, be happy. *I really wanna say, shut the hell up, TMI, cuz you looking dumb right now, even though you probably just don't test well.* I know what you're saying in your mind. Your justification for the person bragging about failing a million times is that the serial failure is just encouraging others not to give up, but to go after the dream no matter how many times you fail. However, the reality of it all is that anyone can take the test whether you're bright or not, therefore, if you fail it 100 times, you get another try and life goes on. None of us are equal anyway, including your doctor or lawyer. One of them graduated last in his/her class. After all, somebody's gotta be last. Chile, if my doctor or lawyer went online and bragged about failing the medical exam or bar exam, I would fire them immediately! I'm rolling on the floor laughing! Some things need to go to the grave. Let sleeping dogs lie. *Teehee.*

The real estate school is a for-profit business. Who really cares if you pass or fail? The only person who should care if you pass or fail is you. Ok, maybe your mom! Moms always love to boast about how their baby passed his/her exams. Other than you two, no one else cares. The real estate school is there to provide the information needed. You're there to figure out how to pass. The instructors give you study materials, practice tests, and go over case studies in the classroom—all of which you pay for in order to become a registered student. So, maybe they do care because they give you a service for your money, but do you know what I mean when I say care? The same goes for the testing site. The testing site allows you to take the test over, and over, and you pay each time to retake the test. They're making a nice piece of change on those retake fees. I wish I had a testing site, I'd probably be rich based on the fees alone! From my understanding, there's no limit as to how many times you can retake the real estate exam. I know that if you don't pass the medical exam three times, you're not permitted to take it again for a year. Even then, the maximum amount of times you can take the MCAT in a lifetime is seven. After seven times, you can *Fuhgeddaboudit! No, I'm not Italian, but I used to live on the same block in Brooklyn as the Italians and we used to go to the meat market and eat the Italian pizza. I grew up with the Mafia…TMI. I was talking about failing the MCAT and got all distracted. Sorry.* What was I saying again? Oh, one of my college friends could not pass the medical exam for nothing. After her third attempt, she decided to become a dentist.

Once you pass the real estate exam, you will need a brokerage or firm where you can hang your license. In other words, because you're not a Principal Broker, you're required to start your career under a Principal Broker. I always get the same question about which brokerage is best. Put their names on cards, throw them into a bowl, close your eyes and pick one. There are just too many firms from which to choose. It's like anything else, it's a personal choice. Each and every person will need to find out which brokerage is best. There's no one-size fits all answer.

Then here comes the next question. "So Claudine, why are you at your current firm?" There are three main reasons why I'm where I am today. Maybe there are four, but for now let's focus on the three. First, I personally like my coins and this brokerage allows me to keep most of my money. Second, I'm a serial student, therefore, education is paramount for me. Since I like to be educated, and this firm offers education like no other, not just for real estate, but for business minded individuals, it seemed very attractive. Third, I own my own company, Dream Girls of Real Estate, LLC.

I'm sure you all know me as Dream Girl Claudine, thus, the name of this very book. Furthermore, because I own my own company, what do I look like promoting another company? The people who do that are the owners of franchises. Starbucks is the first one that comes to mind. If I own a Starbucks, I can't use Dream Girls of Coffee. I own Dream Girls of Coffee, but I can only have a piece of paper that I can hang on my wall. I must, however, promote and continue to brand Starbucks because that's the agreement. I run my operation the exact opposite of this model. The only way it would work for me is if I could open a Starbucks and name it Dream Girls of Coffee and take all the knowledge, training, and recipes then remarket it the way a supermarket does. The supermarket carries tons of brands, but they don't change their name on the outside. Folks have it all backwards. I'd have Starbucks selling me their formula or sending me their product that I'm rebranding. Starbucks says, "Oh no you won't young lady!" This is because Starbucks wants to build their brand, becoming bigger, more well-known, in as many households as possible, yet, you, the little guy, get nothing. You're then working for Starbucks which makes you their employee. *Negative!* When you leave or shut down your location, you're done. Kaputz, if that's a real word.

Traditional brokerages are doing business exactly like Starbucks. You pass your test, you go into the brokerage, they give you two signs and a welcome kit, charge you for a desk and copies, then you get your business cards with their name on it. You don't exist. The reality of it all is that while clients may love a brokerage to death, they usually love the individual, the real estate agent. The agent is the person that makes the firm. They buy from the agent, not the firm. People buy from who they like. They love your service. At Starbucks on the other hand, they really just like coffee. The customers at Starbucks are so hooked, or should I say addicted, that if a barista threw a whole cup at a customer, they would still return the next week. *I happen to be a Starbucks junkie, so I know. Currently seeking help, so don't go judging me. We all got our thing. I guess you'd rather hear me cussing folk out. Naw, I'll stick to the Starbuck drug for now.* Try throwing something at a client during a real estate transaction and let me know how it worked out for you. *Lawd!*

So to answer the question, "Why am I currently where I am?," it all boils down to the fact that I keep most of my money, I'm always learning, being introduced to cutting edge technology, innovative techniques to do business, and I have autonomy to be my own brand. All of those coupled with the fact that I hate to have to pay unnecessary rent when my business isn't done in an office. I despise having copier machine contracts, and managing people is my least favorite part of my business, and lord knows I'm not about to pay someone to manage people. I would have to turn around and manage that person—and there you have my three, plus one, reasons why I'm where I am currently. Nothing is etched in stone. I could awaken to the sun tomorrow and decide I want to make a change, and I can, and if I can, I will. I'm free to fly at any time. Singing, "I believe I can fly, I believe I can touch the sky." *Leave me alone, we all liked the song before the man got charged. I'm not supporting anyone, I'm just singing a song that came to mind. I can't get it out of my head, actually. I've gotta stay on topic.*

Do your research. If there's a brokerage that allows you to keep most of your money in your pocket, offers extensive training so that you have the tools you need, and gives you the freedom to brand yourself, then by all means, that may be a winner. It's best to get recommendations from others before making a decision, but keep in mind, one person's experience may not necessarily be yours. The old saying is, "There's always three sides to every story." What's good for the goose may not be good for the gander. Remember to interview each company and dig into what they have to offer. These companies want you, so please don't go in like you're applying for a job. A real estate agent is an independent contractor.

Never let anyone make a decision for you. You don't have to go there because your mom once worked there, or your great uncle's friend's second cousin first removed was the broker there before he died. Picking a firm is a completely personal decision. There are so many companies to choose from these days, it's a decision that only you should make. The good news is, you're never stuck. If you don't like the company, then you just pick up and walk out, no notice needed, no penalty. There's nothing you need to do but pack up and leave, then email asking that they send your license back to the board. Simple as 1-2-3. In fact, lots of agents jump ship, or company hop, for one reason or another. It's expected and pretty normal. There's a bit of hoopla whenever someone considered a mega agent jumps ship because everybody wants to know why. When a mega moves to another company, we begin to wonder if we're in the right place. *I personally want the Tea. I know it's something bad so I get my popcorn ready. Lawd!* If I leave my company, the world is watching, therefore the chatter will begin and the phone will start to ring. There are numerous reasons why agents leave, personal or professional relationship issues like cat fights or divorces, but the best and most common, is the exit over money! A lot of issues in real estate occur due to cash money. *Singing, "Money, Money, Monay, Monaaaay."* I'd give you some real scenarios but that in itself is a whole *nother* book. Lol!

Any new agent in the business will naturally feel scared as a rookie on day one. The first day is confusing because you're just in the office watching folks walk around, you may have a training class or you may just be organizing your desk wondering what your next move is. My best advice is to locate a mentor, and fast! There's no reason why any new agent in real estate, or any business for that matter, handling the single most expensive purchase of most people's lives should be out in these streets running around without experience. It's a total crime to me. If I were President, I would stop this madness immediately! How does it even make sense to represent a client on a purchase so large with absolutely no experience? Sadly enough, I meet these agents on the other side of a transaction and I eat them alive. I'm a shark and who in their right mind would want to go up against me on a transaction when they have no experience? It's absolutely ludicrous, but I see it every day and I have absolutely no words. There comes a time where one must realize that one can't save the world. *I'm just saying.* What makes matters worse, I can't help the new untrained agent during the transaction. Unfortunately, for the poor new agents, I have a responsibility to my client and my client only. I can't be feeling sorry for the new agent and mess my client up. It's the new agent's seller/buyer and/or her brokerage's fault. I'm doing my job. And that's all I got to say about that. While I can't personally save the world, I do think there needs to be a change. Consequently, this book is my contribution to the world. Don't go it alone. Save yourself the learning curve. Attention, all virgin agents, get a mentor!

CHAPTER 4

What is your WHY?
Who or what do you love?

You've heard this before. It's nothing new, but it's true. You've got to find out your WHY. Why do you want to sell real estate? You must know. When you discover the WHY, then you'll understand why you do what you do. When people run me down to tell me they want to be a real estate agent, I look at them and think to myself, "If you only knew." Instead, I just encourage them to go for their dreams. I often wonder when I'm contacted, "What is it about real estate that makes you want to be a part of it? Here are some of the responses I get in my inbox:

"You make it look so easy."

"I don't really want to do DO real estate, I just want to make some extra cash."

"I heard it was *easy* money."

"I just want to do it on the side"

"I'm not trying to sell real estate, I'm trying to flip homes and invest."

The WHY is very important. If your WHY is clearly defined, then the way you approach this, or any business, will be different. If you just want a part-time gig and it doesn't work out, then there's no real loss other than the class, the fees, and your time. However, if you have five kids to feed and a mortgage, and real estate is your only source of income, then your motivation to succeed will be a bit more amplified than a person who already has a steady income. No different than anything else, the reason WHY will differ from person to person. The WHY is very personal. There are a few cases where the WHY is someone else's, not yours. For example, my grandmother told me to do it. My pastor thought I'd be good at it. Your WHY changes in different scenarios. A WHY could be as simple as eating food. If I'm hungry, I eat. My WHY is that I was hungry. If I just eat to eat, then my WHY is different. Perhaps, I'm going through something and I use food as my comfort. This could turn into eating socially, which could lead to a myriad of different situations. Then there are people who have a burning desire to succeed and their WHY is so different from the person who just barely wants to get by. Success could be something that's expected, therefore making success the WHY. Each person is different as well as each person's motivation.

My WHY is so strong yet simple: I didn't want to be broke. Period! End of story! That's pretty much it, cut and dry. I'm way too cute to be broke, it just doesn't look good on me. I don't know any other way to say it. I knew that I needed money, lots of it, and I needed to be sure that I could provide for my family. I know the meaning of the term legacy and how important it is. WHY for me meant that if I did real estate and was successful at it, I could completely control my life and my future. My WHY made it very easy for me to do what I do. Real estate allows me to have a life of convenience, financial stability, investments, build a legacy for my family, and give back to my community. These are the results, or the answers to my WHY!

My WHY was also about survivorship and responsibility. I have to eat to live and I have a responsibility to those who depend on me. I know who I am and I know what I like. For me, I walk to the beat of my own drum and I do what I want, when I want, and how I want. I loathe the very idea of anyone ruling over my life. It was introduced to me at an early age that I've got to learn how to fish, because when you learn how to fish for yourself, you won't go hungry. Moreover, I will not allow anyone to pick my fish for me, much less feed it to me. If anyone did pick my fish, I wouldn't like the fish no matter how nice the fish was, so it's best that I pick it for myself. I'm particular. *I like mostly wild caught fish, especially salmon, but I do like a good monkfish, shark, shrimp, crawfish, lobster, and crabs too in case you wondered. Alright, you didn't wonder, but you should have wondered. Bwahahaha!*

In addition to being my own person and not wanting to be under anyone's regime, I had a special relationship with money. Money was something that I always wanted a lot of. I can't exactly pinpoint when I started thinking this way about money, but I knew that I wanted and needed it and was going to make sure that I went after it. When I started my first real job on Wall Street at JPMorgan Chase & Co., I was fascinated with money. Money was all around me. I was with money all day. We had a relationship…we really did! I'm so serious. I swear one of y'all are going to send this info to one of those shows on A&E like *Hoarders* or *Strange Addictions*. Get over yourself, it wasn't like that. I didn't go to dinner with the money on dates, but wait, I technically did. You get what I mean. I didn't kiss the money and talk to it like we were a couple. Oh, wait, I do recall kissing money and talking to it. I think I might need help. *Lawd!* Seriously though, money wasn't a new thing for me. Money was my job. I was working at a bank, so go figure. I worked 80% of the weekday and all I did was work around money. If you work in food, you do food. You work in makeup, you do makeup. You work in real estate, you buy homes. See my point? I was buying Yen, trading, buying up CDs. Back then I remember a CD was at 18%. The good 'ol days. Even though I was surrounded by money, none of it made sense to me until I got a little older, somewhere around age 24.

It's funny when I talk openly about money, the reaction I get from people. You should see how they act. I'm weak with laughter just by looking at their reactions. Some are tense, uncomfortable, others are silent. I mean it runs the gamut. There are people who hate talking about money like it's the bubonic plague. Real, living, coherent, people actually hate money. I'm as serious as a heart attack right now. Did you read what I just wrote? It was news to me that people have bad relationships with money, meanwhile I'm over here romancing this money like we're inseparable, like Siamese twins—we definitely are inseparable though! I can't breathe without money.

I once posted on Facebook saying that I was tired of not being a billionaire and this guy had the audacity to come on my post to tell me that money was evil. Then one of my real estate friends told me that he was wrong because the so-called truth is that the love of money is evil. Another guy responded on my post by saying that I was evil for wanting lots of it. Oh my God, people! I was mortified at the way folks viewed money. I began to feel badly for those who were writing negative comments on my post because I knew that there was nothing I could do to change their mindset. I couldn't believe some of us were taught that we should live with either no money, below our means, or just enough. You only hear broke folk saying this nonsense. From a broke person's perspective, being rich is for other people. Wow! I still shake my head when I hear this stuff. People, we need money to live, and lots of it. Lack of money will kill you—I mean that as literal as I said it. If you can't pay your bills, cover your basics, and enjoy the marginal things in life, your stress level alone could drive you insane. Bill collectors are ruthless. *Good Gawd.* When you have a lot of stress over money, it becomes a mental health issue. I know I'd get depressed if I couldn't pay my bills.

There are so many advantages to having lots of money. As a minority individual, there are tons of reasons why I, in particular, must have lots of money. Money for me is freedom and access. I want to help others, but in order to do that, I need lots of money. If I had lots of money, I could make big decisions. I think big, therefore I need money to support my big thinking. Money is power. I like control—of my life of course. *Hell, I want nothing to do with controlling anyone else cuz my life is enough. I can hardly control what I got. I ain't got no time, Chile.* Now don't get me wrong, there are other things I'd like to control—rather not say here—and only money would allow me to have that type of control. I say all of this in a positive way. I'm not trying to start wars, take over anyone else's life, or have a mutiny, I'm just saying that having lots of money could help make things happen that normally wouldn't. Bottom line—you need money in order to be in power and lots of it. I personally need money for my legacy. I have a tribe of great, great, great grandkids depending on me and I'm not about to let them down. *In the South they say, "I an finna let 'em down fuh nobody!"* I take this responsibility very seriously and I won't be a screw up to my offspring and their offspring.

If all this money talk bothers you, then fine, I get it. Sidebar: The people who actually have a hateful feeling towards money are the very same people collecting on

Facebook either by GoFundMe or PayPal for funeral expenses, child expenses, and God knows whatever else when a tragedy strikes or an unfortunate turn of events takes place. Attention Money Hates: Please don't take my advice. If you don't think you need lots of money, just stop reading. Do you, boo! Good luck with that. The rest of you, shall we continue?

You may not believe that I grew up in a basement most of my life until I graduated high school. Yes, I am and was a basement baby. Sounds horrible I know. Maybe I should rename this book, *Basement Baby*. I grew up in a basement in New York City. I said basement, not dungeon. *Lawd!* Some of you don't have a clue what a basement is because you live in areas where homes don't usually have basements, but in New York, it's very common to have a basement. It would be a crime if a person didn't have a basement. Basements are located underground, like underneath a home. Some basements are dark with little to no windows and mostly low ceilings and low lighting. However, basements can be outfitted any which way you like depending on how fancy you want them to be. Our basement was moderate. It wasn't fancy, yet it wasn't subpar. I didn't have a problem with it, but if I could get a do-over, I wish we had one of those fancy basements like the ones I see these days. Hey, it was my normal and I survived so I can't complain at this point. Besides, that was then and I'm thriving as a human today, so no harm, no foul.

Not to bore you with my backstory, which really isn't a backstory, but for the purposes of this book, it's always a good idea to put a sprinkle or two about how it all began. I promise I'll make this long story very short. My parents were immigrants, bought a three-level home in New York, and we lived in the basement. They rented out the two floors above us which was extremely wise of them. Well, maybe they weren't wise. Maybe they had no choice. They had a mortgage to pay, so they had to get someone to pay the mortgage or else they would've been stuck paying it for themselves. Even if what they did was out of necessity they won. They rented the joint out and made it work. The two families who rented out the two levels above us basically paid the entire mortgage, bills, and the sophisticated private school education for me and my four siblings. I guess that ain't too bad.

When people ask me how long I've been in real estate, I can actually say that I was born into it. I just didn't know it at the time, but I realize now that I actually may have been paying attention. They call that unconsciously conscious, I think, because I wasn't subconsciously unconscious or subconsciously conscious. I was more like clueless. Thank God I'm consciously conscious now—I think. Lol!

I distinctly remember growing up in a home, therefore, I knew that there was no way on earth I could live in an apartment. A home was my normal. I just can't stomach the thought of living in an apartment and paying rent. I would always think that if I had an apartment, that anyone could come in my home and that would make me uneasy. I also knew that I wasn't making any money by paying rent. At the time, I didn't even know it was called equity. I just figured it didn't make sense to me. I felt like I needed to be in control over every aspect of my life. I wasn't about to be in a position to have the apartment people telling me what to do. You remember that whole, 'I don't like folks telling me what to do' attitude? Well, living in an apartment would make me feel like I was being controlled by someone else and that wasn't gonna work. Oh, no sir! *Singing, "Control, Now I'm all grown up…..Mona if you Nasty!" Look, don't even ask about the Mona thing, that, again, is a whole nother book. Lawd!*

As soon as I finished my master's degree and graduated, I built my first home. I was young and uninformed, so my grandmother hired me a real estate agent. Since I didn't really want to tell her he seemed a bit old school, I decided to go get my real estate license. Bless her heart. Not sure if you know that the phrase, "Bless her heart" isn't a good thing. My grandmother is with the angels so I can say this now, but if she were alive, there would be no such talk. *I kinda felt something just now. She may be watching me from the heavens. I swear that woman is looking down on me. I just hope she's still proud of me. You know I was her favorite until she got Alzheimer, lost her mind and couldn't remember me. Let my family tell it, she was in her right mind. They thought she knew exactly what she was doing and that she was just acting funny, when clearly that wasn't the case, but they don't listen.* Lawd, look how my grandma got me all confused. Look at karma. I'm sitting here talking about her being confused and look at me. Can we get back to finishing this book? I'm tired. So as I was saying, the Realtor that my loving grandmother recommended for me was old and didn't seem to know what was going on half the time. Nice dude, but a bit slow for my speed. I'm a New York, fast talker, ready to rock and roll and this guy—man oh man, THIS GUY—was moving at a snail's pace. There were times that I didn't know if he was gonna make it through the transaction. I'm so serious right now. You have no idea. He would be telling me about his hemorrhoids and such. This is a true story y'all! I'm not kidding! You can fall out laughing if you want, but I'm dead serious on this one. The man had me weak with laughter half the time, but I didn't dare tell my grandma a thing. She did her part and that was the end of it. I would never dare tell her about her buddy 'ol pal, nope, not me! She loved him and thought he was the best!

The next move I made was to go down and sign up for the real estate class so that I could get my license. I really didn't want to be a real estate agent at that time, partly because my realtor didn't seem to make it exciting. He didn't seem like he was thrilled to be doing his job. He was a retired veteran so he talked a lot about his check and that he wanted to be sure he got his retirement and/or disability check and that it was very important that he didn't make too much money until he was 70 because then, he couldn't get his social security check. I was thinking, "What in the world?" He motivated me to get myself educated about the process so that I knew exactly what I was getting into during this home buying journey. After all, I'd been going to school for 25 years straight since age four, so for me, it was natural to want to be educated, especially given that this was such a big purchase. At no time did it ever cross my mind to become a real estate agent. I just wanted to invest in real estate because my only objective was to build a portfolio for my legacy. I had it all figured out. My plan was to work my regular job and make enough money to buy investments—that was before I woke up. Working a job would not allow me to save enough to invest at the level I wanted to invest. It would have taken me years to gather the money I needed to meet my investment goals. You live and you learn.

Shortly after I received my license, I bought my first rental property. The first is always scary, but once you get past that, you can't wait for the next. I wasn't satisfied with just one, so I started buying more properties, and then the next, and then I wanted even more. More, more, more! I just kept on buying rental properties, and I never stopped. THIS, my friends, is how the million-dollar journey began.

The question then becomes, how did I get started in real estate? When I started as a little chocolate girl in real estate, I picked a small boutique brokerage. I'd built my very first home and was intrigued by the building process, therefore, the new homes division was very attractive to me at the time. Typically, most agents don't start out working in new homes right away. Those jobs just weren't for tan girls at that time. I saw no one who looked like me, and frankly, I didn't care. I decided that I had to do what I had to do and make it work, because when I commit to something, I don't do it to fail.

My office was nice, but it was cold to me. There was no one there with open arms looking to help me. When I walked in the office, it was empty and dreary. Please understand that everyone was very nice, but that was about it. The welcome wagon wasn't standing at the door saying, "I'll help you girl. I see you're new!" It was the days of, "You better figure it out or you won't eat." Let's not forget that I learned how to fish, so I had my fishing rod on me at all times. I was determined to do new construction since I was still working a corporate job at the time and I heard that they needed agents on the weekends. That was perfect for me. *Singing, "Working nine to five…trying to make a living."* With a nine to five, there was no way I could work in real estate during the week other than during my lunch or at night. Look, I was able to hustle that too. I would tell my clients that it's best to meet after 5:00 p.m. because the neighborhoods are active after dark, this way, they would know if they're buying in a good area. If that didn't work, I would find ways to delay them until the weekends. I had this system going well! My job was actually flexible, however, I worked 45 miles away from my office and the traffic going through the tunnel was consistently horrendous. I could never trust that I could be on time for an appointment and there was no way I was showing up to an appointment 30 to 40 minutes late to see a client. That's just not my style.

I actually had my license almost a year before I started selling real estate, mainly because I was lost and confused on how to get started. I kept my job until I figured out exactly what to do. With no help, the learning curve was quite interesting. I would say it was more like a cross between a maze and a roller coaster than a curve. The good news is that I owned a home prior to receiving my license, so I was somewhat familiar with the process. Shortly after buying my first home, while I was finishing up my real estate course, I purchased my first rental property. I got my license, moved from my first home, built another home in which case I represented myself. *Go Me! I was my first deal, but who cares. Why not be my own Guinea pig! Look, I was ready after my first deal.* It was lights, camera, action from that point on.

What really piqued my interest and made me begin wanting to explore real estate was this young drug dealer named Charles. Seriously though, Charles was a pharmaceutical representative—a legal drug dealer. *See, your mind was all over the place. Glad I got you back on topic.* I was walking out of a new home's site and I noticed that Charles appeared frustrated. He had a look of despair on his face. At this time, I had only bought my own home and represented myself. I had no *real* real estate experience, no on-the-job or in-the-field training—none. All I had was faith, and I knew that I was a problem solver. I'm wired so that if someone needs help, I automatically think it's my job to help. I told Charles that I would help him. Inside I was a little uncertain, but what did I have to lose? Charles was already losing, so we could only go up from here. I sat down with Charles, found out what he was looking for, made sure he was qualified, then we literally went hand-in-hand, knocking on doors, until we found a person who would sell him their home. We knocked and no answer. We'd knock and the person said they weren't selling. *In the back of my mind, I'm thinking somebody better come through. Of course now, there's Sales 101 that teaches you not to worry about all the NOs, because for every nine NOs, there's bound to be one YES.* We continue to knock, and finally we come across a home that was actually rented. We contacted the owner, offered them over the market price and, BOOM! Charles bought a home and I was victorious! Charles was my very first client and after that, I knew I could do this business. I was no longer a virgin and I have Charles to thank. *Oh lawd, that didn't even come out right. Forget it. You know what I meant.*

CHAPTER 5

Think like a restaurant, act like a Realtor
Before you attend Real Estate School

Here is how it normally goes, "Hi, I watch HGTV
all the time. I've always loved looking at houses, I want to
become a real estate agent. What school do you recommend
so that I can get my license and start selling real estate?"
WRONG!

Real estate is a business. All along, you've been tricked
into thinking you should go get a license and become a
single agent, then run around and sell a house here and there
and end up broke. Ok, maybe you haven't been tricked, but
that's certainly what I was led to believe. I don't do real
estate as a single agent now so why start as a single agent
when it's very difficult and very stressful? Why do it the
wrong way from the beginning? Please listen to me. The old
traditional way of doing real estate isn't the way I would
recommend you go about doing business. It can cause a lot

of stress. It's a waste of valuable time, and frankly, it makes no sense. This is a bonafide, legitimate business, and should be treated as such. Why not start out doing it the correct way, right out the gate? My advice is that before you go into real estate, please get a business plan just as you would with any business. Simple business principle 101. I don't mean anything complicated, I mean something simple. You can get a template online for next to nothing! You guys are resourceful. If you can't get one, then pay someone. Just do it. It's necessary. You have to
know your numbers. Each person's business plan is specific to their lifestyle so there's no *onesizefitsall*.

Let's for a moment think of a restaurant. When you open a restaurant, there are essentials that you need before you can even open the doors. Let's list them together: A name, location, tables, chairs, receptionist, greeters, servers, food, chef, bar, cash register, bathrooms, lights, cups, forks, knives, manager, napkins, beverages, accountant, reserve funds (contingency cash), employees, lawyers, licenses, advertising, customers, etc. The list can go on and on. You wouldn't even think of opening a restaurant without at least the above, therefore, why would a real estate agent think about opening a business without the necessary essentials?

Let's for a minute think about the essentials of a real estate business. What is your business name? Have you thought of something catchy? You're probably thinking of your personal name. Stop! Nope, not recommended. I don't like personal names unless they're catchy, but it has been done and lots of people think it's great. I knew a girl whose last name was Green and she really used it to her advantage. There it makes sense. I also think the name should be easy to pronounce or easy to spell. I mean, how can I look up a company on the internet if I can't spell the name for goodness sakes? Those gimmicky names always seem to catch the eye and are great for advertising.

All real estate agents should have an office because the brokerage firm is supposed to have a place where you can meet clients, but if you don't have one, you can easily rent a space. You need a place to have meetings, a place to meet clients, as well as a place to put personal items, signs, etc. so that you look *official*. That's what my millennial child tells me I am when he thinks I'm cool.

From day one, before you become an actual real estate agent, you should have a reserve fund. Why is this important? It's a no brainer. You must have money in reserves in the event you have to pay your bills while you're waiting for a deal to close, etc. Usually, it's recommended to have six months, but I say one year is best. I can't tell you what this amount is because I don't know your monthly bills and expenses. Only you know what that number will be.

You need a budget, I would recommend at least $20,000. That's a low number considering that you need the following: signs, business cards, staff, advertising dollars, real estate fees, photography, website, office supplies, start up items. Did you know that real estate fees are at a minimum around $1,900 just to get started? Having an assistant is key to your business. On the very first day you begin your real estate career, you should open your business, day one, with an assistant. While you prepare for your exam, you should be interviewing your assistant. That process alone can take two to three months. Three months of the assistant's salary should be saved in an account. The idea is that the assistant should be so good that he/she will be making you money within that 30-90 day period, therefore creating their own paycheck. The assistant should be on a 90 day probation period. We all know that the assistant will prove him or herself in the first 30 days so you won't need 90 days to know if the assistant will be any good. I can't tell you how critical an assistant is to your business. There are a few things you might be able to get away with, but when it comes to an assistant, I would say unequivocally, absolutely not, NEVER! Would you believe that I have hardly ever written a contract or that I rarely do paperwork? Think about it for a second. Who owns a business, meets their clients, does the paperwork, all the accounting, flips the burgers, writes the contract, closes the home, builds the house, takes out the trash, cleans the windows, does the mortgage? It would drive any sane person nuts! If one person has too much responsibility, then there's no way to offer the level of service that's needed.

A real estate agent is often taught to do everything from the beginning to end when that's NOT the role of a real estate agent. The real estate agent should have ONE real job, and that's to bring in new business. The real estate agent should hire someone to do all the paperwork. The ugly truth is that if an agent is doing all this work from beginning to end, then there's no way there's time to focus on new business. It's better to leverage the work out to someone else which frees up time to go after, and focus on new business. The best part about leveraging that service is that if an agent is smart, he/she doesn't even have to pay for it.

A CPA/accountant is needed because you must know your numbers. The numbers are how you run your business. A good accountant will meet with you quarterly to make sure that you're not overspending in certain categories and make sure that you're never in the red or at least warn you whenever you're getting near the red. You want your business to be profitable at all times.

CHAPTER 6

Now you've got a license!
What do you do next?

The first thing you MUST do is take the necessary training that's required, but that will be explained to you through the brokerage. You'll need to do post licensing classes and training through the local real estate board. You'll want to familiarize yourself with the forms and the documents so that you understand what's needed in a transaction. Next, I recommend you hire a mentor. Don't you dare go ONE DAY into the real estate business without hiring a person who can take you through your first three transactions. PERIOD END OF STORY! If you don't have someone who knows this business, who can hold your hand and take you step-by-step through the process, then forget it. This mentor is not free. Pay the mentor. Offer this person 50% or more. It's worth it. Yes, that's right. If you want to learn, there's a price to pay. If you get lucky enough to shadow a mentor, then you're winning, but the value you get from a mentor who shows you the business is priceless. The real estate business is multifaceted. You can't learn it with three tries. You'd need years of experience and a myriad of clients to even scratch the surface but, a good six clients or so will at least get your feet wet. Paying a mentor to help you through the process will be the best advice I could ever give you. Hands on experience in real estate will beat any classroom tutorial.

Find a person who's been in the business for more than seven years. The reason I chose seven is because real estate is cyclical. After seven years, they should have seen a few things go up and down. Ten would be better, but I think seven years says they've been in long enough to have a bit of knowledge and have the tenacity and stamina to take a few punches that qualify them to be able to mentor you. When I say a mentor with seven years, I don't mean just any old agent with just seven years of experience. Please be sure you find someone who mirrors what I'm about to share.

Next, you've got to get the word out to the general public that you exist. You've got to tell everyone who you are. You should've budgeted for this! You'll need marketing materials, radio ads, television commercials, internet marketing, targeted Facebook Ads, Instagram Ads, Billboards, whatever. Do it ALL! You need to be everywhere, in everyone's face, all at once. You need to dominate the market for three months straight. Then, after about three months, you can begin to pull back. Within these three months, you have to go hard. If you don't do lots of marketing, then no one will know who you are. Marketing materials labeled *"Coming Soon"* are better for grand openings and brick and mortar companies. Real estate companies don't usually do a lot of it, but it can be done.

Next, decide where your business is coming from. Are you looking like a deer in headlights? You definitely want to be sure to create business, any business. No business, then you're OUT of business. Where is your first client coming from? Most sales trainers may recommend that you start with your database. Well, what database? In a way, we all have a database. If you're a Google user, then you have a database. It may not be much, but my Google saves every person I've ever emailed. May not be much, but that's your database if you have absolutely nothing. Your other database is your cell phone. You should have contacts in your phone. My phone is attached to my Google account, which makes my database is pretty large. Folks, BEFORE you get into business, you've got to find a client.

I recommend that you have at least seven sources of business. Don't make the mistake of getting close to that one friend, she sends you all her friends and family members because she loves you, then one day you fall out of love and all your business goes away. Don't make the mistake of relying on bank referrals, then all of a sudden, they decide to divvy up the leads to other deserving agents. Don't rely on your husband's co-workers because he works in the Human Resources department and has all the relocation hook-ups. What if he gets fired? BAM! You're out of business. There are tons of lead sources, but for the purpose of sharing, here are a few that I recommend and the ones that worked for me.

The best people to practice on are your friends and family. *Practice though? I'm not even gonna start with this one, so let me keep writing.* I certainly don't believe you should practice on ANYONE when it comes to real estate given that it's one of the single most expensive purchases of anyone's life. However, the top sales people usually say it's best to start with people you know, like friends and family. I must be the most unlucky person there is, because NOT ONE friend or family member bought a home from me when I was a budding real estate agent! In fact, I don't think any of my friends—all of whom are in real estate—have ever bought, rented, or used me for any of their real estate needs. Needless to say, friends and family may use your services, but I wouldn't rely on their support of your new career.

There's nothing wrong with selling to strangers. Strangers are buyers and sellers too. I use the analogy of McDonald's. Do you think they rely on friends and family to buy their burgers? It would be ludicrous to think that only your friends and family should support you. There are far more strangers than friends and family members. Do you realize that you'll run out of family members before you run out of strangers? There's a new stranger born every day. *Common sense thinking.* Go for the strangers, and go for as many as you can find.

Attention please! Don't be upset with any family or friends that don't support your business. It's not their responsibility to help your business grow. We all want support, but if I don't eat chicken and you start a chicken business, why should I support you? I may be able to tell a friend, but that isn't my responsibility either. I see a lot of posts online about how people don't get support. Your work should speak for itself. If you're good at what you do, then you become a magnet, and others will find you. Great talent need not apply. People who are great are found. If you want support, then you have to work hard to earn it. Support will come when you're so good, that your work will introduce you. No one owes you anything. Life and business is tough and you gotta put in that work. If no one supports you, then find a way and make a way. Where there's a will, there's a way.

Definitely use your sphere of influence. This isn't only family and friends, but we all have people we connect with on a regular basis. Your local place of worship. *NO, I'm not talking about Starbucks or Chick-Fil-A. I can't with y'all.* You may have a child on the soccer team. You may have a friend who works at an apartment complex. You may hang out at the nail shop a lot. Females especially are always getting their nails done. Men go to the barber. All the people you connect with, from your dry cleaners to your gas station could be a part of your sphere. These people know you and may be more willing to give you a chance, or the opposite is true, they know you and would NEVER let you sell them a rotten egg! Lol! Try to find authentic interests to connect with potential clients and referral sources.

Door knocking is a great source. I think we old heads remember the Electrolux vacuum and the Encyclopedia salespeople that used to come around knocking on doors. They had no care or shame. They knocked their knuckles off and they sold those items because I had both I mentioned. My parents must have been gullible or in need. Lol! Groups are also great. Some already belong to groups like sororities or fraternities, but there are business groups like The Chamber, BNI, and plenty others. If you can't get into a group because it's tough, given that they already have a real estate agent, then start your own. My motto is, If you don't get a seat at the table, make your own *dern* table! *Well maybe it's not my motto, but it is something I would have made up had I made it up, but maybe I did make it up. I don't remember where I got it.*

And who cares.

Then there's traditional media advertising. Advertising isn't cheap, but think for a second about those in your area who advertise. I know of a particular furniture store that if they broadcast one more, *Last Sale of the Year,* commercial, I'm gonna lose it! However, notice that I said that I know of a particular furniture store. Their advertising is very effective. It's so good that I've actually visited and purchased furniture. When clients ask me where to get furniture, this store is on the list. Digital marketing is also a great resource. We said Facebook, but digital marketing can go on many devices such as phones, iPads, and computers. Billboards are even going digital through Bluetooth now. Technology is great and it keeps on getting better.

Lead Capture is a great resource that anyone can add to their business website. You can have your website set up so that if someone goes on the site, it forces them to log in after a few looks. You can also add a Pixel to your webpage that'll keep people on your site or retarget them. Ever click on a favorite watch, shoe, or any product for that matter, then all of a sudden you see that same product again? That's retargeting. Nowadays, I think if you are meditating on something, the computer knows. Lol!

As much as I hate to give any love to Zillow, Trulia, or Realtor.com, buyers really do go to these sites first before they buy or sell. Buyers use these sites to see what's on the market, although at any given time, approximately 80% of the homes listed on any of these sites are already under contract. Sellers use it for Zestimates which we all know are false most of the time, but it is what it is. If buyers and sellers want accurate information, they should definitely seek a professional, not a robot. The reason these sites get very little love from me is because the homes belong to my seller, my brokerage, with my name all over them, yet I have to pay thousands, yes thousands, of dollars to get leads from my own listing. If that isn't highway robbery, I don't know what is. It's crazy as hell and we do it. The more you spend, the more leads you get. The hotter your area, the more you pay for the leads. My area is super HOT! If I had $10,000 a month to spend on these sites, I would have tons of leads, but I refuse to do it. I would be spending $100,000 to make $300,000-$400,000. I'll go ahead and say it, I used to use these sites and they got watered down. I was scared to let them go for fear that I would not do well. But *BehBey*, I went cold turkey, let them go, and made a lot more than $400,000 without them. When they tried to win me back and couldn't guarantee me the same number of leads, I declined. Not to say I wouldn't consider them again, but I can't afford to pay them more than $500 per month and by the looks of it, in this area, you have to be spend over $3,000 monthly to make real money. I mean six figures. I decided to find another way to make that, and more, and didn't spend one more RED dime. *Is a dime red? Where did I get that one from?*

Social media platforms like Snapchat, LinkedIn, Instagram, and Facebook are great lead sources. With the 2.5 billion folks on Facebook, it's a guarantee. The thing about Facebook is that you have to know HOW to use it. There's a free way, and a pay to play way, both can work, however, you must have a budget set up to do this effectively. I like the FREE way. I developed a class called, *Market Like A BOSS!* I train and coach real estate agents how to generate leads on Facebook just by making posts. Let me just repeat that it's FREE! And, it works. If you don't believe me, please visit my Facebook page and look at the videos and all the testimonials. I don't make stuff up.

Google Ads I hear is also a good resource. Everyone at one point wanted to be the first listing generated from a Google search and maybe they still do. I have never used Google Ads, but maybe I'll take a look one day. Of course, open houses are fabulous. You'd think that everyone would do these. Are you ready for what I'm about to say about open houses? Before I get to that, let me just remind everyone that new home construction sites have open houses seven days a week! The reason why they're so effective is because they advertise very well and they're specifically looking for buyers. Now here's the twist I want you to understand loud and clear. I host open houses, but I'm not at all interested in buyers. Buyers are internet scavengers. They go online first before they buy anything. Houses, cars, televisions, whatever. The buyer will only come to the house on the second visit. By that I mean, they already saw the house online, so they already saw it. The physical visit, which I call the second visit, is only to validate what they saw online, or to see what the pictures were missing. This is the reason why phenomenal photography is so important.

As for me, when I host an open house, I'm looking for the opposite. I want Sellers with a capital S! I can see your face right now. *REWIND! I can even hear the rewind sound on the turntables as you look perplexed.* I said buyers already know how to find what they want, but the sellers are not online looking for a listing agent, trust me. Not most of the time. They may get trapped into finding one by Lead Capture or by name recognition, perhaps they called a popular company first. For the most part, sellers go with recommendations from neighbors who sold, friends, family members, or maybe they walked into a firm. You may not know this, but most times when a seller is looking to sell, the seller goes online and starts looking at homes to buy. This is what I've found to be true. The problem with my area, is that quite a few of our sellers are relocating to other areas, the sellers are online but they don't really know that they may fall into the hands of an agent while in pursuit of that perfect new home.

So, back to my story about looking for sellers. Guys, this is news you can use. *Yes Gawd!* I try to host my open houses once I get an offer on a property. Oh *Lawd!* I can hear the naysayers, the old agents, the crabby folks, and the like screaming superlatives. I coach real estate agents, so I shared this concept with one of my coaching students and she actually told me that it was illegal! I swear, I can't. If it's in fact illegal to market a home after it received an offer on it, then I would say that we're all illegal agents. Every dang call I get from a Zillow lead is under contract. So now whatchu got to say? I'll wait. For all you guys back there grumbling and mumbling under your breath, I guess you don't know YOUR job. Let me enlighten you since you may be a bit confused. Your job is to market that home all the way up until closing. I know you've had a perfect career where all the homes you've listed ended up at closing, but for the rest of us, there are reasons why we need to market a home up until closing. Things happen, so it's my job to not only market, but market the home all the way until closing so that I can help my clients get backup offers in the event something should fall through. This was sort of my secret, but I decided that I'd share. I used to work in new homes and we would be advertising homes all the time that were under contract because we worked out of a model and we needed something to show. Builders may have five floor plans and one model, so that under contract home helped me sell the new builds. Of course, when a person came in, we had to let them know that there are others that can be built. On the other hand, when you host an open house and the house is under contract and you happen to get a buyer who just LOVED it and would have bought it if it were available, then Booyah! You've got a buyer you can sell something else to. See, it's a win, win!

Back to how I use my open houses to attract sellers. The biggest complaint I hear from my coaching students about why they don't host open houses, is this, "The only people that come to the open house happen to be the nosy neighbors." Ok, it's the same theory or belief that if you have a big forehead, you should accentuate it, instead of hiding it. We can solve that nosy neighbor issue immediately. If we know that the nosy neighbor is coming, why not invite them? This way we allow them to feel comfortable. Not only do we invite them, but we feed them and we offer giveaways. They have always wanted to see what was in their neighbor's house anyway, so this gives them a free invitation to snoop. Some neighbors actually like to see how the homes have changed, been remodeled, or upgraded. This is a good time to give your stager some props, *I guess she gave you props first when she staged the home. IF that wasn't a pun, I don't know what is!* When the neighbors come, what's the very first question they ask? You guessed correctly, "How much is it going for?" If I had a dime for every single time I heard that question, I'd be paid! Unfortunately, we can't discuss the actual offer price, but we can discuss the list price. Of course, they already know it because as soon as that home hit the market, Mr. and Mrs. Crabtree saw everything they needed to know about the house because they were comparing their home to the one listed. You know their house has all the best features, better bells and whistles, imported bamboo flooring from China, corner lot on a cul-de-sac on a hill, with Trump gold hanging from the chandelier. You know the type. Under no circumstance will you divulge the offer the buyer made on the home. If you do, then you're putting your seller in a bad position. So the sellers start pouring in because they heard you had wine and cheese, a raffle for $1000, and a 75 inch TV. *Wow your open houses are off the charts! I barely give water and a mint.* Hey, there are some really good open houses out there. My favorites are the builder open houses. I won $500 at one! Once the neighbors get there, they may ask you the question they always ask relating to the price. Stand erect, poke out your chest, ignore the question they ask and quickly respond, "It's SOLD!" You've gotta love the look on the neighbor's face when he/she finds out the home is ALREADY SOLD! Technically, nothing is sold until it closes, but SOLD sounds so much better than under contract.

Meanwhile, all you really have is an offer. Inspections haven't been done, contingencies haven't been removed, and we haven't even gotten the buyer underwritten, but it sure does sound good. The seller has an extremely high interest. You've got his attention now. He actually starts telling people about you *and* the home. Looks like you created a raving fan without doing a thing! They all want to know the same thing, how much the property went for. You of course can't say, so you ignore the question once again and you reply with, "It's barely been on the market and just like that, we had several folks practically fighting over it. We're actually accepting backups and we may be getting one here soon." I hear some of you complainers again whispering this time. Calm your nerves. There's nothing wrong with what was said. We're accepting backup offers. We're ALWAYS accepting backup offers until the day of closing. Furthermore, your honor, I didn't say we have a backup, I said we MAY be getting one soon. I could otherwise say we're expecting one. I 'm always expecting an offer and a backup! *Now leave me alone. Bwahahaha. I can't.* If you can just place yourself in the mind of the sellers, who only came to snoop around and drink up your wine in hopes of winning some cash and prizes, you would know that these potential sellers are looking at you like you're the G.O.A.T. *Hey, if you don't know what a G.O.A.T. is, please don't be offended. The first client that called me that was a millennial, and it was through text message! I was very confused, wondering, "Why can't I be a unicorn or maybe a butterfly, but a Billy Goat?" How awful. Here's the good news in case you don't have a youngin' handy, G.O.A.T. means Greatest of all Time! These days, I'm calling myself a G.O.A.T. even though I don't like it, I love the fact that Muhammad Ali was called one, and I love to be compared to the greatest! So call me a G.O.A.T. all day, I'll even make goat sounds! Lol!*

What was I saying before I started talking about animals and all? Oh, the sellers are now thinking that this agent is the BEST! You did sell the home in record time and here's the icing on the cake, you're revered as a hard worker, instead of just getting a contract and running off to the next deal, you actually continued to look out for the seller's best interest by marketing the property all the way up until closing. It's a win for everyone involved! The seller has no complaints because you're doing your job, they have a contract with the possibility of backup offers. The buyers may come through and find out the home is under contract, yet that may motivate them to write a backup or they may hire you to find them another gorgeous home. The nosy neighbors, also known as potential sellers, win also. They get to snoop inside their neighbor's house *with* permission, and they have your contact info in the event they want to sell their home. Looks like the agent really wins because he/she comes out smelling like a rose! They've made the seller happy, provided the opportunity to pick up buyers and sellers, while remaining a quintessential professional who sticks with the deal, and goes above and beyond to represent the seller all the way up until closing day. WOW! Winner Winner Chicken Dinner! *I see flashing lights like the blue light special they used to have at Sears, or that Krispy Kreme light. Chile, I'm getting super hungry and I can't even eat sugar on this new diet!*

When inexperienced people get into the business, they think it's best to start off small and spend less in the beginning because they never know what may happen. This is the myth that I want to debunk. When you're starting out, you want to go strong and go hard. You want to knock people upside the head with your advertising. They need to be inundated with as many flyers, advertisements, television spots, radio advertisements, giveaways, you name it! Flood the market, make your mark and then you can ease back a bit. Advertising has a residual effect. You brand them hard and often, then pull back. The audience doesn't count the ads, but whenever they hear it again, they remember because they were whipped with it so much that it became a part of their psyche. Strange how the brain works. I used to have folks tell me they heard me on the radio, yet I hadn't been on the radio in YEARS! Now that's residual for sure. Lol!

CHAPTER 7

Are you a 007 Secret Agent or Are You A Social Butterfly?

I'm gonna lose it if I hear one more person tell me that they don't use social media because, "I don't want to put myself out there like that." *Lawd.* My favorite is when I hear, "I don't put MY BUSINESS out there like that." Honey, you NEED to put your business out there, and all the time! Your business is real estate, not the twerking you did on Saturday night. Folks, it's too late to think you're putting yourself out there, wherever that may be. You're a real estate agent. You *are* a business. Hello, come on out cupcake! Do you understand that once you sign up with a brokerage that you have automatically become a public figure? Facebook in particular is a FREE platform where 2.5 billion plus people frequent on a daily basis. The World Wide Web is where the real estate organization puts your personal information, and there are over trillions of people there seeing who you are. Just Google yourself once you get your license. By law, you must be attached to a brokerage, therefore making you very public. Thus, by default, you are already on social media. You cannot be a business and be a secret. Nothing is more ridiculous than being a secret business. In the past, most businesses wanted to be visible and on a corner. Now that we have the internet, you can be on the corner of the world. Social media has made it so simple that you can be in your pajamas and create a profile of whomever you want to be. You may never actually sell one piece of real estate while fooling the public into thinking you're a billionaire, and they'd never know! Listen, folks believe everything they see. We have folks on Facebook jealous of other people's fake fabulous Facebook lifestyle. I look at Fakebook sometimes and I laugh because I see some of the fake stories being told right before my eyes and I know good and well that it's all lies, but if the public doesn't know, then they just don't know. It's great entertainment. After a while, people become the character they portray on Facebook.

The idea with social media is that if you're not on social media then you're losing the real estate game. Social media is not just Facebook. There are other platforms from LinkedIn, Twitter, Instagram, Snapchat and the list goes on. Facebook and Instagram are very popular and both have business pages, but you do not have to pay to play. On Facebook, if you interact with your audience, you can organically get business. It works and I've proven it over the years. I tell people all the time that I'm outsmarting Mark Zuckerberg at his own game. I'm not paying for ads on Facebook because I'm using my personal page as my business page, in disguise. I figured it out and it works! You just gotta know the trick to it, and trust me, it's not hard. It was a little trial and error, and then all of a sudden, Boom!

The real trick is that you have to first be on Facebook. Please get an account, if you have an account and you're not using it, the least you can do is post once a day. If you're not trying to grow, then stay where you are. The rest of you, please use social media to help build your business! My recommendation is to post a minimum of four posts a day. Ten or more would be best. It's not excessive. One post per hour is just fine. You want to provide a good mix of posts. Try to be consistent. When you wake up in the morning, try to post at the same time every day. My recommendation is that you put up an inspirational post. Post something that'll get the day started. Even something as simple as, "Good morning," or, "Make it a great day!"

Social media can change your business, I'm an expert in the ways that social media can be used to promote and shine a light on your business. My use of Facebook to promote myself and the Dream Girls of Real Estate has created a following of fans, associates, referral partners, and, yes, friends around the world. Too many agents are Secret Agents, never talking about their work and keeping it separate from their real life. This gives the impression that they're less than serious about real estate or that it's just a job. Changing that mindset is key to building a successful real estate business. There are more than 8000 agents on our board, only a handful of them are well known around town. Why is that? It's simple, most agents act like they're 007, they keep themselves a complete secret to the world. I, on the other hand, want to be known as the Best Agent on Earth! In order for the world to know me, I have to put myself out there, front and center. My goal is to be the only person that potential clients think of when they're ready to buy or sell.   Secret agents don't use social media like Facebook, Instagram, etc. They don't wear their name tags around town, if ever. They don't tell anyone that they're a real estate agent, yet they expect success. If no one knows you're a real estate agent, then how could they even think of you when they have a real estate need? The minute you become a real estate agent, you should tell everybody and anybody you meet that you're a real estate agent. Once you tell everyone you know, find folks you don't know and tell them. You can't be shy in this business. This is a contact sport wherein you need to be making contact at all times.

I believe that if you patronize a company regularly, they should do business with you in return. My Mercedes-Benz dealer, nail tech, dry cleaner, hair dresser etc. happen to be my clients. They know me, trust me, and are reminded every time I see them that I'm a real estate agent. The line I use goes something like this, "I'm a little disappointed." They of course want to know why. My response is, "You know I do real estate and I haven't received a referral from you, I know that you know folks who live indoors." This keeps them from saying they don't know anyone who wants to buy or sell. We ALL know folks who live indoors! Unless all their friends are homeless and live on the street, then they DO know someone who lives indoors. Then, I follow up with this statement, "May I count on you to find me someone who's willing to buy, sell, or invest in real estate?" I don't stop there. I end by letting them know that I'll call them in a few days to see if they found someone. This puts them on alert and they start consciously thinking about folks wanting to buy. Eventually they'll attract someone who's ready and call me with the referral. This really does work if you try it out. I'm a master at begging. I have no shame in my game. I try to hunt for business because I don't expect it to fall in my lap out of the sky.

I had a referral for an agent in another state, and for the life of me, I could NOT get in touch with the agent. She had nothing indicating that she was a real estate agent on her Facebook profile page. Her number was not visible and, moreover, I couldn't inbox her because we weren't Facebook friends. I went to Google, found her number, called her and gave her the referral. If you know me, you know I had to ask her why. I just couldn't let it go. I simply asked her why she didn't have any information on Facebook so that folks could easily find her. Her response blew me away. She said, "I don't put my number out there like that." I said, "You do realize that once you become a real estate agent, you're a public figure and your number is on the WORLD WIDE WEB, right?" When I checked her Facebook page, she only had about 400 Facebook friends, yet the web has billions of people who can find her just like I did.

She was more concerned about Facebook when she should have been more worried about someone in the world finding her on the web. Even after I explained that, she said she would consider a Google number to avoid people from having her personal cell. I left that conversation puzzled. I don't think I got through to her, but it is what it is. Every saint has a past and every sinner has a future, so if you had a tainted past, deal with it. We all have ex-friends, enemies, past relationships, and the like. Some of us have that one person we never want to see or talk to again. That's why there's a block button on Facebook, use it. As a real estate agent, you want the world to know who you are and your name. The more people who know you, the more likely you'll get them to pick up the phone and call you for your services. Social media has more than two billion users. Even if that number is skewed due to duplicate pages, that's still a whole heap of people. It's so powerful and critical to your business that if you're not using social media in your business, then you may be losing out on potential business. Let's be clear, however, that being on social media is not the same as using it. I use social media to create champions and raving fans.

CHAPTER 8

Champions versus

Raving Fans

Y̲ou need people on your team who love what you
do and tell everyone they know. Finding those champions
who know everyone, or who have a platform from which to
promote you, then keeping them engaged and on your team,
broadens your audience exponentially. Real estate agents are
like rock stars. Rock stars need champions and fans. In this
business, reputation is everything. If you have no champions
or raving fans, then you're just done. *Put a fork in ya.* A
champion is someone who's gonna cheer you on and tell the
world about you, no matter what. God bless them. If they
hear that someone is selling a roach motel, they're putting
your name out there. Fans are people who really don't say
much, but they love you when you don't know it. They do
rave about you, but they may not always do it as loudly. The

best way to get champions *and* fans is through social media. The majority of champions are your clients, but there are a few champions that aren't your clients, however, they're in your corner, sharing your posts and saying fabulous things about you. The best part about champions, is that you're sure to get referrals from them. One of my champions from Facebook whom I've never met, thinks I'm the best real estate agent in the world!

Fans on the other hand could be anyone, from other agents around the world, family, friends, Facebook friends, and even a few haters. These folks like your posts and engage with you. Some of them don't like your posts, won't share or engage, but you better believe they're watching closely. I'm always surprised when I run into a fan in the grocery store and they tell me about how lovely my vacation to Dubai was. I usually pause and wonder who the person really is because I've never seen a like or any form of engagement from this individual. Basically, this person is a fan or Facebook stalker who watches diligently, but will not press like and will not comment. My sister falls into this category. She can tell you your whole life story, but will not engage or like anything. She will only go on Facebook to keep up with the newsfeed like a stalker, but that's about it. No likes or comments from her, ever!

Whether a person likes or engages with you, they're still watching. As long as you position yourself as an expert in your area, your inbox and phone will be replete with business. I have proof of this because each week I get inbox messages from potential buyers and sellers who are complete strangers whom I've never interacted with and further, didn't even know we were Facebook friends.

CHAPTER 9

How to stay in touch with your current clients
You WILL be cheated on, trust me

Your current clients should never be referred to as past clients or they will become your past clients and they'll be gone forever. Please keep your clients current and top of mind. There are many ways to do this. The easiest way is to keep them on an email list or put them in a Facebook group. If you're not constantly in front of your clients, *Poof!* Just like that, they'll forget about you. Real estate is not the most loyal business. A new real estate agent is born each day! A fresh new piece of real estate meat is sitting on the bench, just waiting for their turn to get in the game. You want to be sure that when any of your clients think of real estate, the first person to come to mind is you. You have to keep yourself in the forefront so that you remain their go-to agent. There is nothing worse than looking up and seeing your client gallivanting around town with another agent or finding out that your current client listed their home with someone else. If this does happen, then it's no one's fault but your own.

Please don't feel bad, just know that you missed the basket. You didn't aim properly and your focus was not on your clients. Conversely, there are those who don't care about loyalty, therefore no matter what you do, they may go elsewhere and there's nothing you can do to stop that. If you did your best, then so be it. You may lose a client here and there, but it shouldn't get you down. It's not the end of the world.

Over the years, I've done a bad job of keeping in touch with my clients so I had to find a way to get back in their good graces. I literally had to thank my clients for sticking with me. The way I just forgot about them, it's a miracle they even remembered me. Then again, I'm so hard to forget, what client could REALLY forget me? I'm all personality! I make the transaction fun and exciting so there's NO possible way that my clients can forget me. I would be hurt and upset if they did forget me. In all seriousness, I have not earned an A+ by making sure that I stay in front of my clients. The good news is, even if you've neglected your clients, you can always open the almost shut door. To rectify this situation, I called each one and asked them if I could update my files with their birthdays and anniversary dates. Whenever you call a client, be sure you have a reason to do so. Small chatter is wasteful and can be uncomfortable. Here's the script:

"Hi Mr. Jones, this is Dream Girl Claudine, How are you? Long time no hear. You've been in that home for almost five years now, I hope you haven't forgotten about me. Just kidding, I know you wouldn't have forgotten about me! I don't want to take up a lot of your time, but I'm updating my new system because I'm doing some great things for my clients this year as it's a milestone year for me. You were definitely one of my favorites! I can't leave you out, but I don't have your birthday listing in my system for some reason, I need to have it so I don't miss your important date. Oh and by the way, do you know anyone moving? Well, can you promise me something? If you hear of anyone even thinking of buying, selling, or investing in real estate, no matter how big or small, will you pass their names along to me or send them my information? You promise? I truly appreciate you. And my promise to you is that I take care of them with the highest level of care that I offered you. Thanks so much for your time and I look forward to chatting with you again from time to time. I hope it's ok if I can check back with you to find out if you know of anyone who may be selling or buying in the near future."

I found that with my schedule, there is no way I can constantly talk to over nine hundred or so of my clients, so what I decided to do, put my clients into groups. For example, I created the Exclusive VIP Facebook Group. This group is not very active, but I post something once in a while so that it has activity. Remember that my clients are already on Facebook and they're my Facebook friends, so they see all of what I'm doing. The VIP group is for specific posts that are ONLY for them. I only post once a month or if something significant goes on because I don't want to inundate my clients with lots of posts. There is a thing called too much social media. The general population doesn't need that information. The point is, if you're not staying top of mind with your current clients, they won't remember you.

Groups are great because you can offer incentives, have contests for your clients, celebrate birthdays, give away gift cards, and keep clients up to date on specific events that may interest them. Not everyone uses Facebook, which means that I can't rely on just the group to stay in touch with my clients, however, everyone so far does have email. One a month I send out an informational email from how to prune the bushes, to how to be safe during the storm, current interest rates, or as simple as a recipe. Anything that'll get a client's attention. In addition, I've been sending out magazines to specific clients. It may not seem like much, but my clients do not throw these magazines out. It has worked where a client called me to sell her home because of it. It doesn't have to be a magazine, but some form of mail is good. What many have stated, when they receive mail, especially a letter or postcard, they usually toss it, but a magazine tends to have a longer shelf life.

My client appreciation events are my favorite! I'm getting better at those each year. I used to just do a small gathering, but one day I came up with a grandiose idea to have a gala. My client appreciation events are off the charts! We wear gowns and tuxedos, give away thousands of dollars, and eat the best steak and salmon. It's such a beautiful affair!

It's not cheap to do, but it's worth every penny! It's once a year so why not? The only problem, everyone can't always make it, and when people don't come, it's a real loss. *Steak ain't no cheap meat, know what I'm saying?* Everyone knows I'm fancy, so I gotta do it big or I'm not doing it!

A gala is not only very costly, but it only includes the adults, and many adults have kids. Some don't come because they hate to dress up and don't want to spend the time to get a dress to attend. Some don't want to leave their kids, or they just prefer a more relaxed setting. I decided it was best to do family fun day, something for everyone. Parents can drink their lives away, kids can jump their lives away, and everyone can eat all the food they want. Face painting, cash giveaways, televisions, fancy trips, bounce houses, music, cotton candy, and so much more. And unlike the gala, the clients can bring their guests. This way, they can bring a friend who sees how well we treat our clients. They can come every year and enjoy us and maybe, just one day they'll consider being our client too. I feel better including the clients, their families and the community. It's a win-win.

I also like to reward my clients whenever I can. If I see a client refer or mention my name on Facebook, or send me a client, I don't care if the client doesn't buy. The fact that they thought of me is worth a million bucks! I'm so flattered when I'm referred. The minute I'm referred, I send a gift to my clients in the mail to show my appreciation. This is a great way to stay in front of the client. I usually get more than one referral from this client because I call to see if they got my gift and then I beg for more business. *Yes I said beg.*

Singing, "I ain't too proud to beg!" In my TLC voice. Lol!

Chapter 10

I eat, you eat. You wash my back, I wash yours!
Building teams and partnerships

Team means, together everyone achieves more. I truly believe that. We work together, we win together. Winning together is how a real team functions. A team looks out for each other and when one is down, the other steps in. I'm fortunate to have a great team of people who work with me. Showing assistants, other real estate agents locally and abroad, ISAs, inside sales associates, administrators, transaction coordinators, stagers, lenders, title companies, painters, contractors and other trades. We can't all be a Dream Girl, but we can build a team whose skills you can leverage to help build your business and increase efficiency. I typically don't have a traditional team. No one is a permanent staple on my team. You can be traded and you can work for anyone you want. I'm the type of person who likes to give people the freedom to do whatever is best. This is why I always have several on my team. If I have one showing assistant and she gets sick, I'm out of business. Why not have two or three? They can show property for others, but they'll also show for me. Lenders are not exclusive to me. I use lenders and title companies, but they also work with other agents. If you do things this way, it's flexible and either party can do as he/she feels. No one feels trapped. Here is the beauty. These teammates get paid per transaction, so they're fighting to get deals closed just like I am. We all have a stake in the game like shareholders, like ball players trying to win a basketball game, you get my drift? People who receive W-2s are a problem for me. I know what you're thinking, I'm just telling it. They don't have the entrepreneurial mindset and some of them will work for eight hours and get nothing done. I need people with drive and hunger who'll work hard until the deal closes. Independent contractors are aligned with the same thinking of a real estate agent and they know that if the deal doesn't close, they won't get paid. The motivation is totally different.

To be a really successful real estate agent, you'll need to build specific partnerships with folks on your team. I happened to learn this later in my career, so thank me now *and* later for giving this information to you up front. Building partnerships is key. Why in the world should I give business to individuals who don't give business back to me? Did you know for years, and I mean years, lenders used me like pimps? I said what I said. They took business, fed their families, smiled, and went about their business. They golfed all week long and didn't even reciprocate. I used to joke and say it was like robbery. How dare you take money out of my children's mouths when you could have shared the wealth? Well, I put a stop to that. In this business we can share the wealth. If I'm sending you business, you better figure out a way to keep me whole. I'm no longer going to send business to any individual who chooses not to send business my way. A referral is not free. We need to learn how to look out for each other. It's so unfair to think how I was being treated. The nerve of some people. I'm angered by this because it's not fair that only a handful of people actually have this information, but when you think about it, if people are good people, they would grow their businesses if they came with an open hand, instead of an extended hand. My advice to anyone reading this book is that the day you begin your business, that's the day to focus on finding all the key people who make your business run, such as lenders, title people, home inspectors, stagers and the list goes on. Meet with them, ask them how you can build together. Once you interview them and find out if they're the right fit, see if they understand the word partnership. If they do, then you'll know they're the one. The day I changed my partners and investors, my business changed exponentially. The taking stopped and those who wanted to keep taking had to go. They were shocked, but they learned that in order to do business with me, we were going to play the game of reciprocity.

All of these businesses should be open to supporting the growth of your business through cross-promotional opportunities as well as referrals. There are a plethora of ways that an affiliate business can support and help you grow. Don't forget that this business is benefiting from your clients and you're the one with the clients. The partnership should be financially lucrative or there shouldn't be a partnership. Each partnership is different, therefore they can be structured differently. In some cases, you may want to partner with a specific company and come up with a marketing agreement. In real estate, you can split the advertising costs in half. In other situations, the affiliated company provides something specific for your clients. Again, there are so many different ways to structure how you can build partnerships with affiliated and non-affiliated businesses. I have asked restaurants, jewelry, and even travel companies to support my clients in the past. They were super excited to partner with me just to be in front of my clients.

CHAPTER 11

All the tea —
The Dark Days of Real Estate

Did you know that just because you meet a client, write up paperwork, and go through all the steps, doing everything in your power to get the deal done, you could walk away empty handed? Yes, with nothing. Not a dime. Nada. No money. You could acquire a $300,000 deal and be depending on about $9,000 of that to survive. Usually it takes about 30 days to get paid that nice piece of change. Most of us have plans for that money, so we've already spent it in our heads even though there's a plethora of things that can go wrong. The buyer could die, the seller can decide not to sell, the buyer can decide not to buy, the buyer doesn't qualify anymore, and let me tell you, this can be because of their neglect or their lender's, but we won't go there, the house burns down or gets damaged, the title work has issues, the list goes on. While you guys are looking at all of the so-called glitz and glamor of real estate, don't be fooled. It's a lovely business, but you have no idea that there are so many horror stories in real estate, I could write an entire book all based on my own horror stories! Where does one begin? Grab a seat and get your popcorn, better yet, you need to get that tea cup cuz you gonna need something to wash it down! Here are a few stories that happened to me personally in real estate that I'll share. There are hundreds, but I'll share just a few juicy ones.

I remember one time I was ready for closing, and the phone rang. A male voice asked if I was listing a home at 123 Elm Street. I quickly replied that it was under contract, and he responded, "Well, there's a truck going through the home!" I could only think, "Please tell me I'm being punked. Where's Ashton Kutcher? This can't be happening!" Sure enough, there was a truck going through the house. A drunk driver drove clean through the house! Left his truck there, took his drunk tail home, slept off the alcohol, then decided to come back after he had a good night's sleep. The nerve of some people! We had to get a structural engineer to make sure the house was sound, a horticulturalist to be sure the tree wasn't going to fall on the home, finally, the fence and siding needed to be replaced. Of course the siding was faded so it didn't match. Of course it was the weekend, and no horticulturist or structural engineer was just waiting by the phone for our phone call. The entire closing was delayed, and now we all had to wait because nothing could be done until we ensured the buyers were whole and happy. Good thing they still wanted the house. If they had backed out of the deal, then the clock would have started over.

The saddest deal I ever had in real estate was when my grandma sent me a deal from one of her closest bingo buddies. She loved this lady to death. She specifically asked me to take care of her friend. That's my grandma, so you know I was gonna take good care of her friend. I sold that house like it was mine. I was proud of myself. This couple was the sweetest! They were moving because their daughter was accepted to a college in Florida, they wanted to sell their home to pay for her college so she wouldn't have any debt. The cost of living is cheaper in Florida. Their plan was to get a cheaper home in Florida and move their daughter in, reduce her expenses and live happily ever after. It was their one and only daughter. They doted on her and she was their whole world. The week before closing, my phone rang. It was a male voice inquiring if I was the agent for the home at 123 Day Street. I quickly responded that the home was under contract and he explained, "No problem, I'm the owner and I wanted to let you know that I…" I interrupted him immediately, "Sir…" He then interjected, "Please give me your fax number and I'll send you the deed." I hung up and began to think it was a joke. I remember pulling over and wondering what my next move would be. I called my broker and told him to look out for the fax. He got the fax and confirmed that the rightful owner was in fact the gentleman on the phone. As an agent who was only in the business for a few years, I couldn't make sense of this. The title search said it was their home. They were paying for the home. They had the mortgage documents. How could this be? Well, while this was very legal, it was morally wrong.

This couple was a gambling bunch and had fallen on hard times in the past. Subsequently, they had made a deal to sign over their home to this company for whom the male voice was a representative. One of the conditions of this agreement was that if they were ever late, they would become automatic tenants, therefore turning over their entire home to this guy, along with the equity. They lost over $200,000, their life's savings, their daughter's future, their legacy, EVERYTHING! I cried like a baby.

My broker, in an attempt to comfort me, kept saying "Claudine, get yourself together. This is not your problem. Your job was to sell the home. What they did with their money is not your problem. You did your job. Stop getting emotionally involved with the transaction." He was as accurate as he could be, but this was my grandmother's close friend. That was the difference. As a result of confidentiality, I couldn't even tell my grandmother the entire situation. I had to avoid my own grandmother! My broker advised me to ask the nice gentlemen if he could give me $2000 so the couple could at least move. He agreed to give me the money if they left it broom-swept. It was the hardest visit I ever had to make. I was lost for words but I had to have the conversation. Those are the dark days of real estate.

You can be yelled at in real estate and disrespected at the highest level by another agent, a client, or anyone in the business for that matter. There are disrespectful people in all professions, but it just baffles me when I see it in our business, because most of the time it's uncalled for. You can represent and work with folks from all walks of life, criminals in disguise, mean, rich people, and the list goes on. I've worked on vacation, while sick, with kids in the back seat of the car, days when I had the flu, even when my foot was broken. I went to a neighborhood with my client and there was a lady yelling racial epithets. My client felt threatened and decided not to buy the home. This being the 21st century, you would think it wouldn't happen, but it does. There's nothing one can do but move on to the next home.

I've walked into homes where folks have been having relations. *Yes Chile...SEX!* Even though we knocked and rang the doorbell, there they were, just having good old steamy sex.. *Lawd.* And you would think that they would stop once we walked in. Nope! They just asked to have the door closed and kept the party going. I can't make this stuff up. I am like, didn't you just see us. Well, when you gotta have it, I guess you ain't gonna let nothing stop you. Folks are bold. I am shaking my head. *That visual though. It sure wasn't that cute.*
Ewweee. If you could only have seen my face. I was Done!

Once I went into a house and I thought there was a dead man present! He was on a machine in a back room and no one notified me that he would be there. I called the agent and went off! It was very scary. Who does that? The guy scared the mess out of me and my client. I have been attacked by animals from cats to dogs to horses, you name it! I once went to show a home and we didn't go in because we heard humans talking at the front door, I wasn't about to enter when I clearly heard voices! It turned out, it was a parrot talking to himself. He was placed near the front door for security, he sounded so human, we thought he *was* human. I've walked into homes and witnessed a gun on the counter when it could have clearly been put away.

You will meet folks who are dishonest and shady. Please remember the rules and regulations. There are people who will try to break the rules and take you down with them. I have had investors try me, clients pull fast ones and other agents do the old, *whisper,* but in every case, I kept my integrity. If you do the right thing, you'll always come out on top. One investor tried to buy an investment property that was only for owner-occupants, so I sent him the federal law in writing just so I could cover my behind. I'm not going down with the sinking ship. I had a client offer me money, so I took the money to my broker, had them take the money and cut me a check, this way no one could ever say I took money from a client. You have to be very careful with real estate. One wrong move and you could end up in front of the board with a blemish and that doesn't look good on your record and it doesn't feel good personally.

Real estate is a competitive market, and there are those that will hate you just because. The next agent is NOT your friend. No matter how much he/she smiles, they are ONLY trying to figure out how to get to the top. I haven't been to an award ceremony in years because no one really cares if you're the number one agent. They really and truly don't care. One year as I was going up to get my award, an agent who didn't look like me was snickering under her breath and a new agent at my table heard it. How unprofessional and mean of that agent.

I'm a superstar naturally, so when I first started at the company I was with at the time, the top agent in the office would introduce himself by saying, "Hi, I'm Greg, I'm the Top Agent in the office!" I don't care what day or what meeting we were attending, this guy would make sure he would introduce himself that way. The next year, he was no longer the top agent in the office so he had to say he was the top listing agent in the office. It was crazy. Being top was so important to people. We used to have contests in our office and I would win all the contests! I won so many contests, I actually asked my CEO to stop the contests because it got really hateful.

We used to have this really competitive contest called March Madness. I thought it was an unfair contest because March is a really hot season for selling. The competition was based on points, for each listing, an agent would be rewarded 20 points, each sale was worth 10 points. If an agent recruited an agent, he/she would get 100 points. When the contest was over, the highest score amongst the agents in the office was 1,100. My score, however was 10,620. I actually gave the entire office a spanking. When I went up to receive my award, the entire room was in shock! I'm telling you, they were all just as hot as fish grease! You would have thought I had stolen someone's baby! For the whole week, there was nothing but chatter about how I cheated and that there was no way that I had scored that many points and that it wasn't fair and that there needed to be an explanation.

The CEO was a nice guy and because he was an African American male who I felt was trying to please the masses, he waited until the next team meeting and decided to explain. If it were me, I would have told them to, you know what! Thank God I was not put in charge. He called me up front and made this ridiculous speech about how I won fair and square because he was present when I won. The rules were 100 points for every recruit. I got a booth at the job/college fair and there were over 1,000 students and staff graduating and looking for jobs and they signed up to be recruited. I was not stupid so I asked the CEO and the instructor from the real estate school to attend so that they could help me. With that many people in attendance, I wanted them to help sell their product too. This was not a one-man job. I also wanted the proof that I was actually recruiting.

Thank the Lord I had evidence or else they may have roasted me alive. You should have seen their faces when they had to apologize for talking so negatively about me behind my back. Some came up to me and mentioned how clever I was, others responded, "I was wondering how you did that." Many of them said, "You know, Claudine is a smart cookie so she is always gonna win." Unfortunately, it was all fake and phony. I was just mad that they were so ugly about it. Anyway, I moved on and waited for the next incident. It goes to show that when folks don't win, they are sore losers, even as adults. Sad but true. The best story of all is when I became the number one individual agent in the office and it was given to an agent who did not look like me. It was crazy! They tried everything to come up with an excuse. They called me a hybrid. They tried to say they couldn't take back the award and asked me what to do. They wanted to know if I wanted a secret award. It was wild. I'm telling you, the drama was crazy.

The worst thing that EVER happened to me in my real estate career is when I had a woman accuse me of being a "Harvard Fake." This woman went on Yelp and social media to discredit my educational credentials and background because she was angry that I didn't purchase a home that she was selling. For the love of God. She tried to make a complaint against me. I had to hire an attorney to go after her and it was removed, but I never got a chance to sue her for defamation. The lawyer took my money and never completed the work. I was just happy it was taken off. Nothing hurts more than when someone discredits your name and it's a flat out lie. The UGLY stuff can be....well ugly, but don't dwell on the negative. Just know that it's there. I never want anyone to think it's all peaches and cream. I try not to dwell on the negative even though it's hard at times. Instead I deal with it, then I purge it and move on to the next.

It takes a whole lot of practice to keep your emotions intact. Keep in mind that real estate is transactional, not emotional. I've developed specific skills after all these years that keep me from getting emotionally tied to a transaction, but every now and then I get human, and those emotions creep up. I have to talk to myself to get myself back on track. Even recently I was NOT paid for over three months.

Yup, three whole months and nothing, Nada. The accountant quit apparently, and the system was locked so I could not get paid. Just think about earning a living, knowing you are owed about $60,000 and you have to sit in silence until "THEY" decide to pay you YOUR money. That is the worst feeling ever. I wasn't really worried about the money so much however, I was worried about the way it was handled. First off, no one offered to help me pay my bills. So that you understand exactly how this went down. I closed on several transactions that were recorded at the city. The wires had been sent to my office. The only thing left was for the wires to be processed. The wires did not get processed because of the accountant screwing up the system therefore I got no pay. As time went on I grew more and more anxious. I had anxiety. I could not pay my bills. For the first time in 17 years, I could not pay my taxes. I had to get an extension which was new to me. I'd never asked for an extension in my whole career. I was given no sympathy, no help, NOTHING.

Finally, one day in May I got some of my hard-earned money. Once I reviewed the numbers, it was clear to me that the pay was incorrect. *I don't know about you but I know exactly what I make because I keep a log of every single dime. I gotta keep up with my coins.* I complained that my pay was incorrect but I was told that it was correct. For fear of being the "angry black woman," I cried daily in silence. I mean I was so sad. I would look at my numbers over and over and think to myself on how wrong this is. I had no choice but to live with it. I didn't have any support. I was tired, broke down, and deflated. I felt like I lost my best friend. I am a fighter of what is right but I really didn't have anything left in me to fight. I knew that God would punish anyone who ever hurt me. You may wonder why I was so passive. Well, that was the same time when the crazy-as-hell lady tried to go after me on line by defaming my name. I working like a slave, the crazy chic was going after me, then I wasn't getting paid. My mind was swollen with stress. I just couldn't fight any longer. I was more focused on getting my name cleared and getting this woman to stop the foolishness. When I get into situations, I usually try to drown myself in work so that I can get my mind right. I love real estate so to get the stress off of me, I just did more real estate. I didn't really have a choice. I also had to make up the money that I wasn't paid. I am very budgeted and to be out of about $15,000 threw me off and messed up my budget. It was time to revamp, recharge and get back in the game. I just gave up on trying to fight.

Fast forward to November, I get a call. This was so unexpected and out of the blue. "Claudine, we owe you about $14,000. We made a mistake. You were right and we were wrong. We will get that check to you this week." Ya think. *This is the effin shit I was saying. Man, I was so mad that I wanted to go postal. When I say that, I mean every single word. I was ready to put ANGRY in the Angry Black Woman that day. But instead, I did the Woosaaah.* I left it alone and said to myself that everyone makes mistakes. I can now focus on other more important stuff.

What I really expected though was that the "sorry" would come with interest. Call me what you want but I darn well deserve to be paid the interest on the money that was

withheld due to someone else's error. The fact that no one offered me any help when I could not feed my family. I lived on my credit cards which means I paid a hell of a lot of interest during that three-month period,. No one even offered to help me pay my taxes. No one offered to pay the penalty I was forced to pay the IRS. The least that someone could have done was to offer me some interest on MY money. NOPE! Not a damn dime. *I was just assed out.* Once again, I just let it go. No fight left in me. I was just happy to have extra money that I had already lost in my head. To me it
was gone and counted as a loss.

      Then it happened again. I didn't get paid on a transaction. *OMG, I am suffering from PTSD or something. My heart is fluttering and I am getting real anxious. I might be experiencing a heart attack. Somebody help me please. This aint good..* I inquire about my pay and get the runaround. All I am thinking is that here we go again. I was silent through the last ordeal but will NOT allow this to happen to me again. For some reason I must have sounded angry when I inquired about my pay. I only talked to my assistant and the owner which turned into me being angry all the time. I hardly ever go into an office and when I do I am very pleasant and kind. I say hello to everyone and I mind my business. I do not start trouble EVER, stay away from the water cooler and never involved in gossip. My only purpose is to sell real estate and be happy.
Oh, and I'd like to get paid the money I earned for the work I put in for Christ's sake.

So I am guilty, I was mad. So what. I should be mad that I didn't get paid. AFterall, I earned it, so I deserve it. I am not asking for a favor. So here's what happened. I sent a text saying that I was being screwed because I didn't get paid. I only sent that text because I felt exactly like I said it. I felt like I was being screwed. I was told that I should not be angry about the situation, that I should give people the benefit of the doubt and that NO ONE but me is complaining. The one that took me right out was this one: When I am upset, it puts people on pins and needles. *I almost turned red and I am not light skinned.* So did I hear this right. *I had to take a moment and listen to the therapist's voice saying, cool your heels, dissect the conversation and carefully craft your response so that you don't regret what you've said.* So I am NOT paid the money that I earned and instead of speaking to the folks who made the error, the best response I got was to shut up, understand that folks make mistakes and by God do not let that Angry Black chick out. My take on it is different. If you mess up my check which is my way of feeding my family, then you should be more angry than I am. And if you aren't then I have no sympathy for you, therefore if you are on pins and needles, then that is your problem. You should be on sharp knives for all I care. How dare someone shame the victim. I can't imagine being raped and worrying about the rapist. I am not at all worried about the person who made the mistake because OBVIOUSLY that person isn't worried about me. And the one thing that I really had an issue with is that the entire office is on pins and needles when I only spoke to two people. I never went around telling folks that I wasn't getting paid. It's none of their business. The other issue is that NO ONE else is complaining because maybe it's ONLY me that's getting screwed. I really didn't think anyone did anything intentionally. but I do think folks should be held accountable. If I were in charge I would be punishing the person who isnt getting my pay right vs the person who didn't get paid.

As a free person, I will not be silenced by anyone. I will speak my mind and tell it EXACTLY like it is, I am not an idiot so people can't just say anything to me and think I am going to go with it. *Don't let the slow look fool you.* When I am right and feel strongly about something, there is nothing a person can do.

No matter what you deal with in real estate, don't let it break you. In any career you'll have adversity, drama and issues but you gotta tough it out and move on. Nobody makes me that angry that I'll lose my shit. *If they don't stop playing with me, they'll commit suicide before I commit homicide. They don't want these problems. Lawd.*

I am a happy individual for the most part as long as others do what they are supposed to do like PAY a sistah. Ijs

CHAPTER 12

The Secret Sauce – Cracking the code
The cat is out of the bag

Everyone wants to know the SECRET! Are you ready? Well, I'm going to share with you right here, right now, the secret sauce to being a great real estate agent, to maintaining a successful real estate career, and to making *MILLIONS* in real estate. It's time to crack the code and give
each and every person reading this book the code to the combination lock. Here it goes…TURN THE PAGE!

Got 'em!

Keep reading….

The reality is, there's NO secret sauce. *I bet y'all were just salivating, dying for this imaginary sauce. Suckahs. Well, I gotchu cuz it ain't no sauce. Y'all slow. You should know me by now. Bwahaha. Why am I so weak right now.* Real estate is a tough business. If we all had the recipe to the secret sauce then we would strike it rich and the world would be a better place. If you know of anyone who has a secret sauce, different from the fact that there is NO sauce, please pass it along because I'm always open to new ideas. The countless number of high-dollar coaches and national trainers have yet to share their secret sauce and they actually charge for their services. If there's a secret sauce out there, it's sure to be worth a million bucks. The good news is, you don't have to pay millions for any secret sauce in this book

To be successful in real estate and in any business, you have to get up, get dressed and do the work. My formula is to get up each morning and meditate. I meditate on the toilet *I get it, I get it. TMI, I know that's what you're saying, but I'm just keeping it real. That is my meditation room. It's really the only place I get peace and quiet away from those kids.* The reason I do this is so that I can get my day straight. I first convince myself that the day will be great. I do a lot of visualization. I sit back and think about how many buyers or sellers I will meet. I set up meetings and I answer texts, emails, and start on my phone calls for the morning. I decide what type of day I'm going to have. If you don't decide what type of day you're going to have, then the enemy will decide for you. Each day is like going to war, so it's best to determine how things are going to be so that it ends up that way. In the event the day goes a bit off track, at least my mind is set up to expect nothing but good things. How you start your day is a good indicator of how it will go. This is why I wait until everyone is gone and I meditate in my quiet time alone. It's a beautiful thing. *Yes Gawd. Peace and quiet. Ain't nothing like it.*

I believe in setting goals and working hard to meet those goals. I'm very focused. If I say it, I gotta do it or I will literally kill myself until I achieve what I set out to do. All of my goals are written down. It helps to look at my goals each day as a constant reminder of what I'm aiming for. Having a *never give up* attitude will go a long way. There is no way I am giving up on myself. The best thing I ever did was believe in me! Giving up on me is not an option. I've said it before and I'll say it again. I'm not in the business of accepting failure. I can't live with myself as a failure. I hate everything about the word fail. Just the "F" alone makes me cringe. *May I have a W for the Win Alex?* I have intrinsic motivation. I don't necessarily need encouragement from others. I encourage myself and act as if I'm my own cheering squad. If you create this imaginary squad, you will be amazed. It's like your alter ego, your very own Sasha Fierce. It's important to be proud of your accomplishments and celebrate your wins no matter how small.

Entrepreneurs are sort of in a bubble. As a CEO, you're not only at the top, you are the top! You may not be in a position to get encouragement from others, so never forget that you must be willing to be your own cheerleader! A winning squad of one!

In addition, you must have passion. When you're passionate about something, it makes a big difference. If you asked me to skydive, I might do it, but I can tell you now, I'm going to have anxiety the whole time and I'm not going to enjoy it. I won't fail, but I'm not passionate about it. There is no way I can even think about working in a field where I do not feel genuinely passionate about the job. I don't care what job it is. Passion goes a long way. My motto is *Let your passion be your paycheck!* It doesn't matter which career you choose, you can easily be the best in that career and be compensated very nicely if your passion does the work. Passion is natural. You can't teach passion. It's like a technically trained singer going head to head with a passionate singer. The singer with the passion, the one who wants it badly, actually sounds better than the trained singer. The trained singer may deliver a composed, yet lackadaisical performance, while the singer with passion is giving us all they have, leaving their whole heart on the stage, taking us to a place where we almost cry real tears. That's passion. When it comes to real estate, I do it with my whole heart. It's not a job and it's not what I do, it's Who I am. I am real estate.

The secret is not in a sauce. The secret is in the agent. Whatever you're willing to put into the business becomes the secret. We all have a different secret. Whoever has The Secret Sauce, please reveal yourself! The vast majority of advertised coaching classes and training seminars are not going to guarantee you any services because the reality is, there is NO secret. There's no secret to making millions either. There are systems. There is no shortage of money. There is however, an increase of excuses and lots of ignorance.

CHAPTER **13**

You can only serve one God
Put all your eggs in one basket!

One basket diversification is the key to growth, success, and sustainability in a real estate business. A combination of passive and active income coupled with long-term planning, will help ensure financial stability throughout your real estate career and beyond. Warren Buffet will tell you the same thing. I'm no Warren, but I am smart enough to listen. When there's a singular focus, success in inevitable. Let's look at Serena Williams, Michael Jordan, and Michael Phelps for example. These individuals only focus on one thing. They are great athletes. Can you imagine if Serena were playing tennis and basketball? I could guess off the cuff that she would not be number one. To be number one you have to go hard and you have to be focused on One Thing. Trying to juggle two sports is going to take the focus off of one. One of the sports will suffer because giving them both your equal time and effort would be impossible. You couldn't possibly serve both fairly and equally, just as you can't serve two Gods.

It ruffles my feathers when real estate agents tell me that they're going to open a few side hustles when they're failing at real estate. *Wait, I don't have feathers but you know I meant. Cliches are something aren't they? I am the master at messing them up. Has something to do with being a foreigner. I think they are funny to be honest.* My response to them is that if they put the effort they have into the real estate business then they wouldn't need a side hustle. I have no desire to sell makeup to make a small margin when I can make $10,000 to $30,000 per sale at one given time. In my mind, it's less effort and less parties involved. *Lol!* If you truly love the business of real estate, you can literally stay close to the business and take advantage of all it has to offer. I've always thought it would be a good idea to master different areas of real estate. The more knowledge you have the better. You can always stay focused on the one area that you specialize in most, but having knowledge in the other areas makes you more knowledgeable than your cohorts and allows you to become more marketable. Just imagine your business card. My business card is too small to carry all of my specialties. If I could I'd wear a digital screen on my forehead so I could display all of my designations. The reason why this is important is because the vast majority of most agents don't have as many designations, and most definitely don't have a degree from an Ivy League school—although not a requirement, it sure looks good!

Real estate has so many sides to it. There are affiliate businesses to consider for extra income streams: Timeshares, property management, commercial properties, luxury real estate, investors, real estate support, photography, staging, real estate closing gifts, contracting, flooring, creating products for realtors, the list literally goes on and on. Selling makeup and jewelry is cute, but the money you are accustomed to making is a better use of your time and effort. Besides, it's related to what you already do, so it makes sense. Think of yourself as a one-stop shop real estate agent. That would be quite impressive. People can't take a real estate agent seriously when they're doing nine different businesses. It looks unorganized, dysfunctional, and confusing to the consumer. Your clients want to know that you're focused and that they're getting an expert rather than a jack of all trades.

CHAPTER 14

Will you bust your skull if you jump off a high-rise building? Failure is overrated

By now you know that I have a different way of thinking. It may not be how most people think, but that's why I regard myself as a unicorn. When I hear phrases like, "You gotta fail to win!" or, "You will never know success until you fail!" I get stressed out. That's like telling me that I have to jump off a brick building to know that I'll crack my skull. *What I'm not gonna do is take that advice, silly goose.* No one is that slow. To experience success, you don't have to experience failure. I am not buying that and that's probably because I've got that unicorn thing going on. Maybe it's an average person thing. High-level thinkers don't go around accepting failure as part of their DNA. Nope. The best one is, "Everybody fails!" They do? Why do they fail? Who are they? I don't know about many of you, but I must be in a category by myself, because failure to me is worse than death. I have no desire to look at myself in the mirror as a failure. I was born to win. I was reared to win. I grew up in

110

an educational setting with winners. I have been successful in my mind all my life. I graduated with high honors from high school, college, then ended up with a master's degree from an Ivy League. Uh, failure, I don't do failure well. As a matter of fact, I don't like the way it looks. We are enemies. If I fail, then it sure wasn't because of me. It would've been because I was drugged up, manipulated or something.

I don't understand why some people are comfortable with failing. People who fail probably fail because they gave up, they didn't do things correctly to begin with, or they're comfortable with failing. I do think a lot of people give up when times get hard, not just in business, but in relationships and in life. If you have a problem in any situation, you should seek out a solution. If you plan well, when you find yourself in a bind, then you'll have a contingency plan. Seek to win, speak life, make the right choices, stick with the goal, rework the plan and keep pushing. Don't let failure defeat you and win. You have to be determined. I don't want to fail, so I do everything in my power to make sure that whatever I say I'm going to do, I do it. When I plan to execute a task, I will do it with all my might and all my power or die while trying. I'm the type of person who, if I'm supposed to do something and I broke my foot on the way there, I'll show up, do what I have to do, then go get the foot wrapped in a cast. Most failures would just call and say, "I broke my foot and I'm not going to make it." I know that analogy is a bit extreme, but it could be a bleeding finger and a failure will come up with why they can't do something they were committed to doing. Most of the failures I meet don't consider others while they're making bad decisions, even when it will affect another person's whole life. Maybe failures don't have vision. I don't understand why people lack the vision to succeed, but for me, I actually speak everything into existence. I don't see myself as a failure, therefore I can't fail. I wake up winning every single day! If you see yourself as a winner then how could you fail? That to me is the key. You must have confidence in yourself that you can be successful daily. It's a daily commitment. Encouraging oneself is very important. Winners don't wait for encouragement from anyone. They know that you gotta get up every day with specific goals in mind and achieve them slowly as you build towards achieving the end result. I don't know anything about failures. This is purely guesswork guys. I can only assume that failures have unrealistic expectations and they go in without having their ducks in a row.

Winners are winning from the beginning, so they're set up properly to win from day one, whereas maybe failures go in blindly hoping for the best. I have no evidence to support the reason why failures fail, however, I do have lots of evidence to support why winners win. The failures that I've met seem to fail all the time and the common thread among these failures is that they all have a million excuses and it sure seems like they all seem the same. They always seem to come back and have these great stories to tell. My question to the ones who love to promote how well they failed is, "Why did you fail when you could have stuck with it?" There's a saying, "Failure is easy," so let's NOT give up for a change. I hear the word failure from so many people that I think it's just a great cliché for promoting books and success stories. Let's face it, it does sound sexier to hear that someone failed at life and picked themselves up by their bootstraps, compared to a story about a person who lived a consistently successful lifestyle. The latter is boring I guess. I personally like to hear from failures though, because if they can tell me the mistakes they made, then I can avoid those, so they're very valuable. The people who we rarely hear from are the winners. Their stories aren't as sexy so they don't tell them. This is true. And thus, this book ALMOST never got written for fear of not having an underdog story.

CHAPTER 15

Bon Voyage – Life after Real Estate
Time to smell the roses

We all throw around the word *million*. Well, it's overrated like everything else. What is a million if you don't know what to do with it anyway? The truth is, it's NOT what you make, it's not what you keep, it's what you invest! Now what? Where are your savings, retirement funds, stocks, life insurance, annuities, rental properties, business investments, products, etc.? Are you gonna sell your practice, pass it along, what will you do with your book of business contacts, franchises, and proposals? Too many agents don't create a long-term financial plan that allows them to sustain their lifestyle into retirement. With a variety of strategies, I show agents with successful businesses how to start thinking about ways to generate passive income to finance an active and lucrative retirement plan.

One day you're making all this money in real estate and the next you're done. You're getting old, you look around and you wonder, "What am I going to do?" Uh, it's too late. You should have been planning for this moment all along. There's no reason why you shouldn't have been thinking about your exit strategy while you were in the real estate game. So let's rewind. Why is it that top real estate agents make on average $100,000 per year? Remember I said top agents. These agents work in the business for approximately ten years. That means they've made over a million dollars. Ask them how much of that money they've invested. All of them I can bet you will say they have lived a pretty nice life. They've taken trips and they have nice cars...at least the ones I know. I'm one of them. I began to talk to some of these agents in my travels, specifically during yearly conferences, and I wanted to see how they were doing with their money. I know their numbers because we're an open book company, so there's no hiding who makes what. After learning that the majority had NO savings, no residual, and no investments or rental property, I nearly fainted. I mean, NONE! I was beside myself. Some would brag about profit share, but that's not guaranteed. Profit share is money that's earned based on another person's production. I found it unbelievable that real estate agents making the kind of money that they were making did not see the necessity of buying and investing in the very thing that they sold on a daily basis. Who better to take advantage of the one thing that they have at their fingertips? I couldn't understand it.

I often notice that there are five critical practices most agents are missing. Unfortunately, not having these practices prevents many agents from being able to retire when they would like, if at all. Without these critical five, most agents will end up pretty much broke and confused. I remain in utter shock at how many successful real estate professionals remain in the business for decades, make tons of money, but don't have two nickels to rub together. I can tell you that on the outside, it seemed as if they lived a life filled with the best of what money could buy, but their retirement portfolio was bare bones, just like a skeleton. *Hell, some ain't even got that. I know of a few that have nothing, Nada. Just a hope and a prayer.*

There is no excuse. When I meet broke real estate agents and hear their stories, I mean excuses, I want to say, "Sistuh, what in the world were you thinking? You must be immortal. Uh, didn't you know that you were gonna get old and need some cash?" Goodness gracious! I can only shake my head in disbelief. *Lawd.* I know some of y'all are thinking you'll rely on your kids. I know my kids ain't wiping my butt or changing my diaper, so I've got to get it together. They're gonna be too busy to be visiting me in a nursing home. I'm doing what I gotta do so I don't need to be worried about that. I'll just pay the professionals to clean me up, hope that my nursing home buddies are my besties, and we can all be in the nursing pen together; old, happy, and thankful we all we got. I can see me now, bossing them old people around with my two-piece bathing suit, dark shades, and big brim hat. Shoot, I might be old, but I'll still be HOT. I'm just saying. Where was I? Oh yes, back to those five practices:

1. Have a clear vision of what age you would like to retire, and a plan to get there.

2. Write down your plan as a daily reminder. If it's written, it gives you a visual of what to work towards. This should be a complete blueprint that predicts about 12 months of monthly expenses so that you can retire comfortably in about 15 years.

3. Know exactly what your monthly debts are, and how much you need to make to pay down your debts. This will allow you a better opportunity to build your retirement portfolio, and accurately calculate your net worth.

4. Maintain a minimum of five lead sources and a way to turn those leads into business so that you can make enough money to cover your yearly expenses.

5. Hire a great CPA who can go over your profit and loss statements for each quarter. If you have a great accountant, they will sit down with you so you can know your numbers. If you don't know your numbers, then you're essentially broke. Rich people know their numbers.

CHAPTER 16

Real Estate & Relationships
Ride or Die

Relationships in real estate can be tricky. If you are highly successful in real estate and making a lot of money, that means that you are working a lot and I mean a lot. Some of us can't turn it off, which means that in order to have a successful profitable career, it is imperative that you have a "ride or die." In all seriousness, if you do not have a supportive partner, then just hang it up. Your relationship could be short lived if your partner is not on board or understands the grind.

The real estate career can be tumultuous therefore your partner must understand that you will be busy most of the time and that could be uncomfortable is some relationships. An entrepreneur thinks completely different from a regular 9-5er. When both are entrepreneurs then things flow much better. The entrepreneur has flexibility but not availability. The 9-5er is off on weekends and ready for family time meanwhile the entrepreneur makes most of his/her money on the weekend. Instead of your partner understanding your hustle, your partner is upset and feeling neglected. That right there is NOT gonna work. The minute that happens, then you are on your way to divorce court. I am simply keeping it real because I have seen it. *Hell, I tell him, you either want a broke wife who cooks and is home all day or a rich wife who hustles and is busy most of the time. You choose. Lawd.*

To me, the best relationships that I have seen are ones where the couple is equally yoked. You know, like Beyonce and Jay Z. They are in the same business so it makes it easier for them to understand each other. They kinda speak the same language…you get what I am saying. It sucks when you come home from a long day of real estate drama and your partner doesn't understand or care about your real estate soap box. This is true of any profession. I know for a fact that I don't understand physics so me understanding that language would be different than if we both were into physics.

This is my advice before you run down to divorce court is to communicate. Talk to your partner about what it is that you are trying to achieve. If you plan to hustle hard, you don't have to do it for the rest of your life. I recommend you set a goal and put a beginning and end date on it. For example: My goal was to buy 10 rental properties over 10 years. I started in 2011 and by 2021 I should achieve my goal. It's now 2019 and I have 10 properties. I am actually ahead
of my goal. *Knowing me I wasn't gonna just meet no goal. BeyyBay, I am on my way to exceeding that. Yes Gawd. Go me.*

When you sit down and talk to your partner about your goals, be realistic. Ask permission to achieve these goals. See if your partner is on board. If it makes sense and your partner loves you then you are winning. If you have a Debbie Downer Doubtful spouse then your relationship is probably doomed regardless. What I find is that many entrepreneurs have big goals and it can be hard to get a partner on board. Let's say you tell your partner that you are planning to hustle for 10 years to achieve 10 properties, but you have not been successful and have a bad track record of achieving goals, then yes, your partner may doubt you. On the other hand, if you are highly successful and your partner doesn't have faith in you then you are really going to have to have some hard conversations. It is hard to believe in other people's dreams, especially if you don't have vision.

Believe it or not, it could take you a while to convince your partner so that he/she believes in your goals and dreams. What I did was put my goals down in writing, shared them with my husband and began working towards them. I grind hard, so it's nice to have a spouse that can cook, clean and take care of the kids. I do not like the gender roles. If I am home cooking, cleaning and taking care of kids, then that interferes with my ability to kill it in the real estate game. I cannot focus on all those aspects of life. Just like I don't expect my husband to change oil and cut grass. What works for us is that I hire a chef. I hire a housekeeper. My husband gets the oil done at the Mercedes dealer and we can get the grass boy to cut the grass. The gender roles can really destroy a relationship.

Society can really mess people up with defining who does what. The old days of "Leave it to Beaver" are gone. I personally hate domesticated tasks. It would kill me to sit at home or be behind a desk all day. Try your best not to assign roles to your partner regardless of your upbringing or past relationships. Especially female roles. Females who have children have a lot of pressure already. Parenting is an arduous task for any gender, but mothers have a special "thing" whereby the connection they have with their children is different from that of a man. Men you wouldn't understand. Sorry. I just don't think some men understand what women have to go through and to be fair, maybe they won't because they aren't women. *So let me get this right Sir. You want me to wake up at 5:30 am, get kids up, get lunches packed, drop kids off, get myself together, work all day, pick kids up, take them to activities, do homework, cook dinner, do the laundry, prepare for the next day, serve you dinner when you get home and then "get on my knees." Imma shut the hell up before I cuss. Boy you done lost your entire mind.*

Some women in real estate make significantly more than men, especially those who are married to 9-5ers. That trend is growing as women take over the world. *Men are cringing at that statement, but get ready cuz here we come. Singing, Who runs the world, Girls.* When the woman makes more money than her partner, the dynamics of the relationship are different. The egos have to be checked on both sides. Men sometimes have a hard time with that. Not all men, but lots of men. Again, it's only because of the societal norms. Men are taught to provide and protect so staying at home or not making enough money to provide can feel strange to "real" men. A man usually wants to be the "head of the household," the one who brings home the bacon. *Those leachers looking for a shugah momma don't even get what I am saying.* The woman is supposed to take the bacon and cook it so we can all eat.

Some men are not yet comfortable with being stay-at-home dads. It's just not cool. Some still believe that it's the woman's job. We all know that there are men who just can't get a job making more than their female partner yet they are struggling with the idea that they make less. At times, they have to take a posture of being in charge to feel better. A woman who gets her own check has a different posture too. She is less likely to need anything from her husband and that can be very interesting.

Imagine if your partner came to you and said he or she were going to become a top recording artist, quit a good paying job and began spending the savings on this new career. *Oh my, that would set me off and the fight would begin.* The odds of becoming another Bruno Mars or Madonna is slimmer than becoming a successful real estate professional. I use that example because you can't get a partner on board with unrealistic goals. I want to also add that if you are in year three of your goals and you have not proven that your hustle is working towards your goals as you promised, then you will definitely lose trust in your partner. You may need to regularly remind your partner of the goals so it is important that you are consistently working towards them.

Failing to meet the goals you promised your partner and expecting your partner to have faith in your is ludicrous.

Once your partner is on board, then the relationship will work out smoothly. If it doesn't, then I don't know what to tell you. *Listen, I have never said I was a relationship expert. Y'all prolly need counseling & this mighta been the icing on the cake. This ain't no bulletproof formula, so don't read this, try it and then blame me cause Y'all crazy. Y'all know Y'all had all kinds of issues that ain't got nothing to do with real estate. Boo Bye.*

Each person's relationship is different. You could be the baddest real estate person on the planet and your relationship could be strained. Those of us who work hard deal with all types of issues because some people do not get the grind. Do not let that stop you. You may have to adjust the relationship. It depends on how bad you want it. I know it sounds harsh but nothing should stop your hustle. If you can't get a partner to understand your grind, then maybe that is not your life's partner. There are facts that must be faced one way or another. *I say, try to find your "ride or die" partner as they call it in the Urban Dictionary.*

I think it is a personal choice. Relationships work because people choose to make them work. The first argument isn't a sign of trouble. Most people whether married or not have disagreements, therefore married folks are no different. Nothing should come between you and your partner when you have a solid bond. Many of my real estate friends are divorced. We can't blame real estate entirely because divorce in itself is high regardless. Jumping ship could mean that the grass isn't that much greener on the other side. I say stick with the person who was there with you when you had nothing, build and grow old together so that when you look back on life you can appreciate the fruits of your labor. No man is an island, without the support of your spouse or partner, you may not have been the successful real estate professional you are today.

The bottom line is that many of us make excuses when it comes to real estate and relationships. You can make it work as long as you have upfront discussions with your partner. No relationship is the same. No relationship is perfect. Moreover, there is no blueprint for the perfect relationship which is why we are pretty much on the trial and error journey of our lives. What is good for one relationship may not work for all relationships. Find out what works for you and your partner. Communication is the key. When you communicate your goals and ideas and solicit support, you should be fine.

CHAPTER 17

Eat like at Gorilla
Real Estate can be Good or Bad for your health

All this talk about real estate, wealth and money is cute, but without a good, solid, healthy, happy, whole person, it means nothing. I'd be remiss if I didn't write one chapter about taking care of oneself. Sometimes we get so caught up with the day to day routine that many of us forget to take care of our mind, body and soul.

If you'll allow me to be completely transparent for a moment *Lawd, when did I start asking for permission from folk? Hell, I've been transparent the whole book, so it's too late now. You can practically see right through me now. lol* I can share a personal story that no one knows about the time I was literally at death's door. *Warning, there are some gory and gross details, but it is what it is. Besides, y'all gotta get it straight or else you won't get the full impact of the story so I ain't leaving nothing out. Ijs.*

In 2011, I was going along as I normally do and noticed that my body was changing. In 2012, I noticed even more changes. I began having a menstruation for over 7 days. Of course, nothing too alarming, so I kept going along with my regular routine. In 2013, my family suffered an awful tragedy that changed my life. I noticed that my period was lasting longer than 10 days. These were heavy periods. I was bleeding longer and longer causing me to wear up to 3 maxi pads at a time. I would not sit for very long periods of time because sitting down would cause the pads to fill up quickly. I wore dresses and skirts mostly to avoid worrying about the pads showing. I really wasn't paying attention to myself because I had two young kids, a very busy schedule, a business to run and a household to attend to. I was all over the place trying to be superwoman.

Let's quickly fast forward to 2015. At this point, my menstrual period was lasting over 20 days. You would think that I was alarmed or concerned. Nope, I made it my new normal. In my mind all I could think was that I am getting older and my body is changing therefore I had heavier periods. When I tell people, they think I was totally crazy for thinking it was normal. Here is what I learned just recently though. I am meeting a multitude of women who suffer with the same problem. As women, we think we should deal with it and not fix it. Why is this I ask? *Heck I don't know why I am asking when I don't even know why my country tail didn't get help.* My only guess is that we just don't recognize the severity of it.

A strange thing happened to me at the end of 2015, something that I could never even imagine would happen to me at my age. I went to a photoshoot right after changing my pads, sat down to get makeup done and all I could feel is globs of blood gushing out. At no time did I think that it was gonna fill up the pad, but I knew it was a strange and uncomfortable experience. When the makeup was finished, I proceeded to get up and to my surprise I destroyed the chair in someone else's home. Yup, the blood leaked out from my menstrual pad to my undergarments, through my skirt and on to the chair. I was MORTIFIED. I was most embarrassed. I had extra pads, but I didn't have extra clothing. I looked at the cloth chair thinking to myself how I could make it right, meanwhile I have an outfit full of blood. I am a grown woman and I had an accident such as this. I can't remember having an accident at least not since High school. No way Jose. This was not happening. Not to me.. I knew that this was a sign that I needed to make a change. It became urgent all of a sudden.

Not only was I bleeding longer and suffering with some heavy cramping, but I was tired and sleepy all the time. In my head, I just needed to slow down, get some coffee and B12 vitamins. Unfortunately, I drank as much caffeine as possible and took the B12 shots. My internal medicine doctor suggested a CBC Blood test. To their surprise my iron level was equal to that of a dying person. I was at a 4 whereas most people are at 15 or higher. The doctor as so nervous that he redid the test. The nurse said the doctor was talking about an infusion and more. The doctor prescribed iron pills and asked me to follow up in 4 weeks. I did everything I was told, went back to get retested and STILL the low iron. We are all perplexed but yet no one thought about female issues. My next stop was a gynecologist. The doctor that I have is super medication happy. She wanted me to take birth control pill to control the bleeding. I refused to take any medication let alone birth control bills. I kept probing for answers and finally she recommended that I get an ultrasound. I go into this room and lay on a bed and they take this penis-like thing and insert it into my vagina. The results showed that I have fibroids. I have no idea what any of this is. I heard ladies talking about it but had no clue. Now I am worried about myself. All I can think right now is that I have cancer. My doctor explained to me that it's common in black females and there are options. She said that most women get a hysterectomy, or they have the fibroids removed. My doctor remarked to me that she didn't like hospitals and surgery. Her recommendation was that I take a Lupron shot. It sounded good to me so I begged for it. She told me all about the shot, it was not invasive, and if it worked, then I would be cured. The shot was designed to artificially push me into menopause. Once I get into menopause, then I would no longer have fibroids. All of my friends have already been through menopause, so they are living the life without a period. I am older than all of them and I'm still walking around with this red friend. Some of you are slow and didn't get it so I'll explain. Red Friend is aka the Monthly red menstrual period we all know and love. lol

Lupron was working out very nicely until I got these dragon flashes. Yes, I felt like a dragon. The hot flashes were the worst. I was dying inside. There was nothing I or anyone could have done. The hot flashes were killing me. I am hot, cold, up and down. I just want to get rid of this feeling.

Here I am in 2016, I visited my internal medicine doctor and find out that I don't need B12, yet I need iron. I meet with my gyn doctor and she suggested that I take lupron or birth control pills. The suggestions were not working out for me so I left it along until one day I went to lunch with a friend. We sat for about 10 minutes and then I realize that I cannot sit for more than 20 for fear of the pads getting soaked and leaking out in a restaurant. When I told my friend exactly why I wasn't going to sit for very long she began to probe me and that's when I told her that I was bleeding. She got into help mode, listened to me and then gave me the name of her doctor. My friend told me that she had the exact same issue and now she is fine. She said that her doctor performed a very simple procedure and she was cured, stop bleeding and now lives a happier, healthier life.

The day came for me to meet Dr. Lewis. He tried to show me a few videos and explain the process. I cut him off immediately because I needed to get this surgery done as soon as possible. *I ain't got time to be wasting with videos. Come on Doc, let's get this show on the road. Snip, snip, chop, chop Buddy. Get to work.* I know the doctor was saying to himself, "this chick ain't playing. He had his assistant set up the surgery, I went in, came out, and drum roll please: Presenting, A Brand New Me. *Yes Gawd.*

Life is precious and in order to live well, we must take care of ourselves. We live on average 80 years on earth. We have only one body which I refer to as a temple.

Unfortunately, the masses of us are uneducated on what to put in our gut. Our gut health is so bad that many are one happy meal from a heart attack, diabetes or high blood pressure. Sadly, the food and drug administration is not of any help. Nutrition just like money management is not taught in school. How to read a label requires a master's degree. The facts are that if we all got better educated, we would all have a garden and start a revolt against the food and drug folk. Ever wonder why it's not the food and DRINK administration? Stop and think. What correlation does food and drugs have? Uh, none other than they both go in your gut. The drugs are NOT designed to cure. They are designed to treat. Doctors are there to "Practice" medicine. The pharma folks are in business to make money. The food you eat is poison and the drug you will need to take can keep you alive for a pretty long time. A lot of kids and adults are on medication for a long time. Haven't we all heard of ADHD, High blood pressure pills, chemo, diabetes drugs like insulin? These are all curable, yet we are dependent on drugs. If you change your gut health and drink only water, eat home-grown foods, home-cooked foods like veggies, remove processed items, alcohol, sodas, all animal products, eliminate ANYTHING white in your diet namely milk, salt, sugar,
flour, potatoes, bread, rice, *I hear all of you saying that I sound crazy. Ok then, do you Boo. Keep staying sleep. You'll get woke once you get sick and you try to rely on the white coats to find a cure to that pain.*

Switching gears a bit over to the elephant in the room. No one feels comfortable talking about mental health. I wasn't either until I had a nervous breakdown, fit, anxiety attack, panic attack, whatever you wanna call it. I do believe that any one of us can be susceptible to having the above-mentioned attacks. I thought a panic attack was something other people had. I never thought it could happen to me. I am fairly healthy and in complete control of myself so there was no reason for me to suffer any attacks much less an anxiety attack. It shocked the mess out of me. I was so scared that I was sending random texts to some of my friends asking them to look out for my kids. *Shoot, I thought I was having a heart attack and this was gonna be it for me. I almost was dumb enough to give up my passwords to my back accounts. My Goodness.* At first, I was shy about sharing my situation but I figured I should let others know because just like my anemia there are other people suffering with the same issues.

My doctor asked me if I had a therapist and the answer was no. I didn't think I needed to talk to anyone but in truth we all need someone. I am not one to share my personal business with anyone, not family or friends. I do what I have to do, deal with it and on to the next. I stay focused on being focused so that no distraction can take me away from my day-to-day operation of Hustling. This method obviously wasn't working for me. It ultimately led to a trip to the hospital with a 180/98 blood pressure. My normal blood pressure is 120/70. Please do not be afraid to seek help if you have any issues at all. Even if you don't think you need a therapist, try to force yourself into speaking to someone monthly or once a quarter. The techniques you can learn from therapy can help you cope with some of the daily encounters. You can be going along on your daily routine and here comes the devil named Susan. *No offense if your name is Susan. It's just an example cupcake, so untwist your face.* If you remember what the therapist said at the very moment Susan rears her ugly head, your response would totally different than how you'd normally respond. I've learned how to respond after I cool down and thoughtfully craft my words. The tongue is like a sword. *And God knows mine can cut you so deep, you'll think you got shot with an AK47.*

My advice is that we are all human and life can really be heavy at times. There are ups and downs in personal and business relationships. We deal with kids, family, death, births, issues, crime, accidents and we also deal with other people's problems. Why we take those on, I really don't know but we do. All of life's experiences become who we are and there are times where we can feel like the weight of the world is on our shoulders when in reality, it really isn't. It's all perspective and how we see things. It is crucial to your health to see a therapist who is trained to help you through life. You do not have to do this alone. Seeking help is not taboo. We all need help at some point so don't wait until it's too late. We've all seen strong, healthy, happy people commit suicide. Our response has been the same, "I can't believe it, she/he was strong and looked like they had it all together. Now you know, it wasn't all what it appeared to be. The look of depression is often hidden under a smile. GET HELP! It won't hurt.

Would you believe that many people do not go on vacation? I mean no travel or excursions. I found that hard to believe. There are people who have never left the city they were born in. I am baffled by this information, but it is true. I love what I do therefore I am on vacation every day. I never need to escape my life's work. I can't live without it. Vacation for me is an excuse to go see homes in other places outside of where I live. I can't wait to see the real estate in other cities and countries. It excites me. The folks who hate their jobs NEED a vacation away from work. I think that when you go on vacation you experience life outside of where you are. It opens up a world of culture and difference. Staying in one place make your provincial, one dimensional if you will.

No one said that you have to be Dora the Explorer, then again, maybe I am saying that. Just get away from your environment and smell the roses. How boring would it be to be born in a city, never leave the city and then die in that city. Go on a stay-cation but do something. Meet other people that are not like you.. You gotta see the world. Getting your knowledge of the world from television perpetuates stereotypes and often the information is so far from the truth. Traveling to other places will enrich your life. If you haven't tried it, then make it a point to visit somewhere, anywhere. Traveling is good for your health, not to mention what it does for your mind. People think travel is expensive but it's cheaper than you think. There are deals all the time. *You spend money on stupid stuff like Starbucks, weaves and sneakers so you got the money. Stop talking crazy.* If you budget and make it a priority, then you can afford it. Just like anything else, when you want it, you do it, otherwise you make an excuse.

Take time for self is very important to your health. There are times where you just need a mental health day. NO kids, NO phone, NO work, NO family, Nothing. Just a day of rest and relaxation. Women are guilty of taking care of everything and never thinking about themselves. The ones who have children are the most guilty. If you have kids and you don't get a break then you are no good to anyone. *When momma ain't happy, the whole house ain't happy.* Women are often left to take care of kids and work. When men go to bed, they go to sleep. When women go to bed, they stop by the kid's room, the kitchen to be sure the lights are out, they prepare for the next day and who knows what else. How can you function for your children and family if you aren't right? *Singing Lauren Hill's, How you gonna win when you ain't right within.* If your home life is jacked up then it trickles into your work like. It all starts running together. What I did was leveraged my life. I hired the housekeeper, cook, assistant, you name it. There is no reason to make good money and live stressed out when you can easily get help. It takes a village. Leveraging is definitely good for your health.

When I talk about health and food, I get the same if not worse ignorant responses that I get when I talk about money. Goes a little something like this. "Chile, you crazy, I need my meat and potatoes."

Or my favorite, "The doctor said that wine is good for you." Or the best, "May grandma lived to be 104 and she ate all that and she's good." Last one, "Nothing is wrong with any of it if you do it in moderation. you will be extremely healthy. In other words eat like a gorilla. You need brain food. Notice I never said exercise. Do gorillas exercise? (Listen to them saying, "I ain't no gorilla." *I can hear you. You know I got ESP. Lawd*

Real estate can be good or bad for your health. It's really up to you. How you manage it, is the key. Try to live a good healthy lifestyle. If you are not strong in this business, you will right about losing your entire mind. Being an entrepreneur in itself is not an easy game, but I'd rather work 25 hours a day for myself than 9-5 for someone else. *Honey, the only reason I'm still sane is cuz I don't work for anyone else. Lawd, they would either fire me or I'd quit after a while.* Me and the job thing just don't get along. I need my freedom.

There's only one you, so take care of that You for YOU! Only YOU matter.

You can't live a healthy life when you have a messed-up mind, body and soul.

CHAPTER 18

Epilogue
This is who I am, not just what I do

I've been in real estate for 17 years and, believe it or not, I've purchased a total of 15 properties. I own nine now, two of which I was forced to sell, and the other four I'm still angry at myself for selling, but you live and you learn. Hopefully by the time this is published, I'll have ten properties. ,My plan is to retire and live off of the rental income. It's called sowing. I was mentored early on by a man whom many of you know named John Burley from the book *Rich Dad Poor Dad.* My big takeaway was knowing which quadrant I needed to be in. I also learned how to borrow money and have other people pay down the debt so that I could benefit. The best way to do that is through rental property. It's a win-win for all. Folks need a place to stay. I need a long-term investment. Love it. The best thing about rental property is that I get all the benefits. I don't have to pay for the property, yet I get all the tax breaks, I get all the equity, I keep the property, and I get to build wealth. And if

I don't want it, I can sell it. Even if the market tanks, I can still rent it out. If the stock market tanks, I can't live in a stock. We all live indoors our whole lives, so rental property was the only sure bet for me. Do what is best for you, but for me, I saw absolutely NO risk in real estate. Yes, there are those who have a horrible experience but again folks, it's called systems. A good system will overcome obstacles and the fear of investing in real estate. I actually wrote a book titled,
Removing the Fear of Investing in Real Estate.

I'm all about my work and I love the real estate game, but don't get it twisted. As much as I love selling real estate, carefully read the next sentence, and read it slowly and carefully please. There's nothing wrong with selling real estate, but you don't become wealthy selling real estate, you become wealthy owning it. He who has land and property has generational wealth. I think real estate agents should own the most property on earth. Real estate agents have real estate at their fingertips. It baffles me the number of agents who don't own, but we're all different, and we do things differently. It is what it is.

There's a new buzz going around called economic extinction in the black community. What it boils down to is this, there's evidence that blacks are losing economically over time and to date, there are indicators that blacks are not building wealth at the same rate as other cultures. While blacks have lots of buying power, they fail to acquire property for several reasons, including bad credit, lower paying jobs, and student debt. Blacks remain consumers and not investors. By continuing this pattern, these behaviors become generational, which is why it's important to share that one of the best ways to build wealth is through home ownership. There are other ways, however, we all live indoors therefore, it's a safe long-term investment. With no money invested, families are turning to Gofundme or Facebook to pay for funerals and emergencies. I'm thinking to myself that I've got to do better. I decided that if I didn't come from a wealthy family, that wealth should start with me. I made a commitment to my great, great, great grandkids that I would leave a legacy. That's very important to me. I've done well, but I want to do so much more because I feel like I can. I'm never satisfied with just enough. I'm going to keep growing bigger and bigger. What's the harm? Wealth is there for whomever wants it. Money only changes hands depending on who has their hand out and who reaches for it.

My goal was simple. I said if I buy ten rental properties starting in 2010 using other people's money and finish buying them by 2020 (last one being cash), then I would pay them all off by 2040, my residual income would be $25,000 per month. So far I'm on track. My lowest rent payment is $1,450 per month and my highest is $1,900 per month. Rents go up each year. So by 2040, my lowest rent will be over $2,000. Yup, I'm on track. I think I can live on $25,000 per month. That doesn't even include my other income. I have my social security, stocks, annuity, and IRA if I choose to pull it. So folks, If you're a real estate agent, please use your money to sow. You don't want to be sixty years old and be out here trying to sell real estate with a cane. That is not cute. You should be at bingo somewhere with the rest of the old ladies wearing your tan knee-highs, and orthopedic shoes with the rubber bottoms. Ok, maybe you'll be at the Tiki bar on the beach in Jamaica sipping on a martini, waiting for your butler named Dexter.

I needed to make sure that I was going to have millions of dollars, and I didn't have a clue on any good way to make a million bucks, so I decided to open a Verizon Wireless franchise. In my mind, I was going to open several stores around my town and make lots of money. I thought my husband would help me, but he didn't seem like he wanted to manage, so I decided that I couldn't manage alone, so I only stuck to one store. My real estate business was booming and my store business was only bringing in one third of what I was making in my real estate business. As a result, rather than hire someone to run the Verizon Wireless franchise, I got an offer to sell it, so I did. I then went hard and heavy into real estate and to my surprise, the market was going downward. An unexpected crash was coming and no one knew. Thankfully for me, I was a go-getter and I didn't let a crash stop me. I was focused and decided to work with new construction workforce housing. I sold more homes than anyone in the middle of a crash. At the time, I was holding on to every penny because I didn't know what to expect. I had money from the sale of the business which gave me confidence and security. One thing about me. I can't be cash poor. I try to keep six figures on hand at all times. If you have assets, such as a few rental properties and you fall on hard times, all you have to do is pull out some equity. If you have to sell one, which should be a last resort, it's yours to sell. I never recommend selling. The point is that your properties have value which allows you leverage. They become your bank. In my business, I try to keep $50,000 in cash, a $50,000 line of credit, $50,000 in reserve funds, $100,000 in an IRA, $100,000 in annuities/stocks, not including millions in other assets such as property, bitcoin, jewelry, and gold.

If we don't share the same interests, you can find other ways to stay connected to the real estate business besides selling real estate. You may want to teach real estate classes. You can do online courses, create class materials, continuing education workshops, etc. Think about writing books, instruction manuals, motivational materials. Creating products can be a great source of residual income for a retired real estate agent. Once you have worked in this business, your career is a valuable asset to the generation coming behind you. There's so much to share and learn at the same time. I think that newcomers can learn so much from those who have been there from the good old days, therefore, it's a healthy marriage of both worlds, old and new. You can also invest in real estate companies, REITs or Real Estate Investment Trusts, and you can even take advantage of profit share. There's a guy in my office that receives fifty percent of his book of business. He still maintains his books from the golf course in another state. He has no license in our state, but he refers business in our state and gets a referral fee. That's the way to go. Leverage is the key. You can even sell your book of business if you'd like because people will buy it, especially a new agent with no business. Trust me, you won't be smelling any roses if you don't properly plan for your retirement. You'll be standing at the door at age 70 with a cane in Walmart as a greeter. Time slips away rather quickly. I look at all the money I've made in real estate and I too should have put away more, but I was in my right mind during my formative years. I'm more conscience now, but aren't we all once it's too late? Lol!

Finally, here's the good news, YOU HAVE ME! I had NO one. There was no one who was willing to tell it all. No mentorship, no help. There were no coaches you could even pay at that time. Now the world is your oyster. The internet is at your fingertips. People like me are here to share. So much information is bleeding through your veins. There's no way you can fail at real estate these days.

If this is the career path you choose, go for it, go hard, and enjoy it. Smell the roses while you're alive!

Claudine-isms

❖ Oh Gawd

❖ Lawd

❖ If you didn't come from a wealthy family, then a wealthy family should come from you.

❖ Love you, because if you don't, then nobody else will.

❖ How could you expect someone to love someone who doesn't love themselves?

❖ Your opinion of me is NONE of my business.

❖ I mind my business and drink my water.

❖ Freedom comes when you don't have to worry about anyone else's opinion.

❖ There's enough sun to tan us all.

❖ LISTENNN!

❖ Working for something you don't care about is stress.

❖ Working hard for something you absolutely love is called passion.

❖ Speak it into existence.

❖ No negative vibes. Move along.

❖ No matter what they say about me behind my back, they're lying if they don't end it with, "She's a beast at what she does though!"

❖ I can, I will, and I must.

❖ I specialize in making things happen. That's all I know.

❖ I'm winning cuz I'm not competing.

❖ Today's forecast is 100% winning.

❖ Happiness is a choice.

❖ Rise and grind!

❖ Best thing I ever did was believe in me!

❖ Lord bless my hustle, double my income, and reduce my stress.

❖ Stay focused on being focused.

❖ It might be raining, but I'm going to create my own sunshine.

❖ I've got dreams that are worth more than my sleep.

❖ Just a good woman trying to be a better woman, while helping to inspire other women.

❖ I'm always busy. I'm building a brand and an empire.

❖ Expect nothing and you'll never be disappointed.

❖ Make your passion your paycheck.

❖ You're only confined by the walls you built in your head.

❖ Shout out to the chicks that get their own checks!

❖ The most influential person you will talk to today is you. Be careful what you say.

❖ I refuse to give up on myself.

❖ I NEVER lose, I either win or learn.

❖ No alarm clock needed. My passion wakes me up.

❖ Sit with winners, it will be a different conversation.

❖ I wanna be blessed so I can bless others.

❖ My biggest fear is being average.

❖ I haven't got anything else to do with my time except win.

❖ Remember that person that gave up, well neither does anyone else. Keep going.

❖ We all have the same 25 hours 8 days a week.

❖ If you're the smartest person in your circle, then you need a new one and FAST!

❖ I'm on the SOOOOoooollllllllllldddd Train!

❖ TGIF: Thank God I'm fabulous!

❖ Today is a great day because I said so.

❖ If it doesn't make me happy, make me better, or make me money then I ain't got time.

❖ Not everyone in your circle is in your corner.

❖ I don't think outside the box cuz there is NO box.

❖ Don't expect people to understand your grind when God didn't give them your vision.

❖ I'm an Earth agent. I can assist you anywhere in the world.

❖ Whether you think you can or you can't, you're right.

❖ You can't teach the grind. You either have it or not.

❖ Always expecting great things to happen.

❖ People will be in secret competition with you and STILL be losing.

❖ Success comes in cans not can'ts

- ❖ It doesn't matter how many people do what you do, they can never outdo you at being YOU!
- ❖ Count your blessings, not your problems.
- ❖ Sexiest thing about a woman is her hustle.
- ❖ If you're not doing what you love, you're wasting time.
- ❖ Stop getting distracted by things that have nothing to do with your goals.
- ❖ The fact that you're not where you want to be should be motivation enough.
- ❖ The only BS I need is buyers and sellers.
- ❖ Some people are destined to succeed while others are determined to succeed.
- ❖ Giving up is easy, let's try sticking with it this time.
- ❖ Don't be upset with the results you didn't get from the work you didn't do. Duh.
- ❖ If you want something you never had, then you better go do something you've never done.
- ❖ Think while it's still legal.
- ❖ Call me crazy, but I love to see other people happy and succeeding.
- ❖ You can't start a new beginning, but you can make a new ending.
- ❖ Clap for your damn self, this ain't no Grammys.
- ❖ TGIF: The grind includes Friday!
- ❖ If you do something you love, it's passion.
- ❖ Only billionaires need sleep.

❖ I'm so tired of not being a billionaire.

❖ You can't deposit excuses, last I checked.

❖ I'm just saying.

❖ It's your Dream Girl Claudine.

❖ Call me Queen Claudine.

❖ A job is a bribe to help stifle YOUR dream so you can build someone else's.

❖ You can do anything you set your GRIND to.

❖ Have goals so big you feel uncomfortable telling small-minded people.

❖ Today I will do what others won't, so tomorrow I can do what others can't.

❖ I'd rather be tired than broke.

❖ God may not be done with you, but I am! Hasta La Vista Baby!

❖ I don't stop when I'm tired, I stop when I'm done.

❖ Successful people do what they have to do, regardless of whether they feel like it or not.

❖ You can't be excellent by accident.

❖ How bad do you want it? Then go get it. Just do it, like Nike.

❖ If it's important to you, then you'll find a way, otherwise you'll find an excuse.

❖ You will want to give up…DON'T!

❖ Life is better when you're laughing.

❖ Stop complaining, we all have a story. Who cares anyways?

❖ Your energy introduces you before you even speak.

❖ Appreciate good people, they're hard to come by.

❖ In order to be successful, your focus has to be so intense that folks think you're CRAZY!

❖ Giving up for me is NOT an option. I will do what I have to do or die while trying.

❖ I'm a Goal digger.

❖ Check your surroundings.

❖ Sleep is not an option. I got goals.

❖ All I know is HUSTLE. That's my power.

❖ I am a unicorn. Cut from a different cloth.

❖ If you can't find a way, make one.

❖ Motivate YOURSELF! You're an entrepreneur.

❖ You're not born a winner or loser, you're born a chooser.

❖ Happy is the new sexy.

❖ Waiting for a sign, then this is it! Get moving cupcake.

❖ Drama doesn't just walk into your life, you either create it, invite it, or associate with people who bring it into your life. Change your circle.

❖ Your confidence will make some people uncomfortable.

❖ A day without selling homes is like….. Just kidding, no such thing. Real estate is my oxygen.

- When you love it, it's not work. I live it, breathe it..it's who I am.
- Winners focus on winning. Losers focus on winners.
- Work hours. Eyes open, eyes shut.
- Best way to predict your future is to CREATE IT!
- Every day is not just a regular day. It's another day to create new opportunities and a chance at a new beginning.
- Energy is contagious. Get your energy right.
- I'm mindful who I allow in my space. I gotta have good vibes ONLY.
- You can't have a million-dollar dream with a minimum wage work ethic.
- We rise by lifting others.
- Real women don't do drama, they do business.
- Your goals don't care how you feel. GET UP!!!
- My smile doesn't mean that.
- You either make excuses or make it happen. Sow now so you don't end up as an old lady greeting at Walmart.
- Trust your dopeness.
- Surround yourself with positive, good people.
- Too many fail because they worry about the opinions of others. STOP IT! They don't matter.
- Givers must set limits because takers don't have any.
- If we don't inspire, motivate, or support each other, we have no business being in contact with each other.

❖ Excuses are for those who DON'T want it bad enough.

❖ Be in love with your life..Every minute of it. You only live once.

❖ Create a life that makes you want to jump out of bed in the morning!

❖ When women support each other, incredible things happen.

❖ If you have no edges or real eyelashes, then you should not be talking about other people.

❖ If you don't know the difference between Your and You're, then we have no business being friends.

❖ It's not how much you make, but how much you make a difference.

❖ Be a professional, classy, person with a little hood and a lot of God in you.

❖ There are hidden blessings in every struggle.

❖ You don't need a reason to help people. Giving back is important.

❖ Gratitude is the best attitude.

❖ Woke up and realized that I don't have what it takes to be average.

❖ Never NOT working.

❖ Don't be mad when I pull a YOU on YOU!

❖ I say what I want because I'm FREE!

❖ Teach people how to treat you.

- When people show you who they are, believe them, then Run! Don't look back.
- You will be too much for some people…Uh,those are not your people.
- It should never be about the money…chase the passion and the money will come.
- I'm not a workaholic. I am a loveaholic. I love what I do and when you love it, then it's really not work.
- One day or day one. You decide.
- Girls just wanna have FUND$!
- I love taking long romantic walks to the BANK.
- My life isn't perfect, but I appreciate all my blessings.
- Girls compete with each other, women empower each other.
- No matter how you feel, get up, get dressed, and show up.
- I can't stop, won't stop. My great, great grandkids are depending on me.
- I will do what others won't do so I can have what others can't have.
- Do you Boo!
- Service before self.

ABOUT THE AUTHOR

With a Master's degree from Harvard and more than 15 year as a real estate broker and investor, Claudine's resume is quite extensive. Her goal as a real estate practitioner is to serve her clients, put their needs first and give them an outstanding buying experience. Mrs. Ellis is extremely passionate about the real estate industry and strongly believes real estate is an extension of who she is.

Claudine Ellis has been one of Coastal Virginia's Top agents since the inception of her career. Her accolades are numerous, but to name a few: She has been recognized by many organizations and has earned the Top 100 Award, Woman of Achievement Award from ACHI Magazine, Quadruple Gold Award from Keller Williams. She has been recognized by the HRRA Association where she received the Circle of Excellence Platinum Award as a Top Real Estate Producer, the Longevity Award for 10 plus years of success in the business and the Diamond Award-the highest award achievable for agents who produce over $10 million in new home sales. Claudine was recently named the #1 individual Platinum Agent in Hampton Roads and the #1 Individual Agent in her real estate office. As a Top Agent, she has successfully earned over $500,000.00 in Gross Commission Income annually. Mrs. Ellis had the honor of speaking on stage in front of a National audience at Inman Connect and was featured in recent news articles for Inman News-the most trusted real estate news organization.

Education is paramount to Claudine's success, therefore, she stays on top of her craft by constantly pursuing real estate designations so that she is abreast of the current changes in the industry. In addition to being a Licensed Broker, she has earned the following designations:

- Licensed REALTOR®
- Accredited Buyers Representative (ABR)
- Certified Luxury Home Marketing Specialist (CLHMS)
- Certified New Home Marketing Professional (CMP)
- Certified Residential Specialist (CRS)
- Certified New Homes Sales Professional (CSP)
- Graduate REALTOR® Institute (GRI)
- Master Certified New Homes Sales Professional (MCSP)
- Master, Institute of Residential Marketing (MIRM)
- Certified Distressed Property Expert (CDPE)
- Short Sale & Foreclosure Resource Certification (SFR)

Mrs. Ellis has earned a Master's degree from Harvard University and Baccalaureate degree from Norfolk State University.

Claudine's level of success has positioned her to be well sought after. She is in high demand for public speaking, mentoring, coaching and training. She created, developed and teaches the "Market Like a Boss" seminar all over the country. Mrs. Ellis is the author of "Removing the Fear of Investing in Real Estate". Moreover, she has appeared on the Builder Radio as an expert in real estate. Each month Claudine is featured on 2 major TV stations in Hampton Roads as the Coastal Virginia Real Estate Expert.

Claudine is very involved in the real estate community as well as the community at large. She served as a former member of the National Association of Realtors, Chair of the New Homes Council, an active Board member for Hampton Roads Realtor Association, Keller Williams Agent Leadership Council and was on the Board of Governors for the National Association of Home Builders. Mrs. Ellis is licensed to teach by the Department of Professional Occupational Regulations (DPOR). She is a real estate instructor for Moseley Real Estate School and is excited to announce that she is in the process of opening up her very own real estate school called Earth Agents School of Real Estate.

Giving back to the community is extremely important to Claudine. She formed a nonprofit organization called Dream DAP, Inc. to benefit those single parents needing down payment assistance. She was a volunteer director and videographer for the Voice of Revival program broadcasted world-wide for over 15 years for Calvary Revival Church. Additionally, Claudine volunteered at the USO on Little Creek Military Base serving the Military Troops.

Prior to falling in love with Real Estate, Mrs. Ellis was the owner of a Verizon Wireless Franchise in Virginia Beach, worked as the Director of Admissions at Hampton Roads Academy and held the position of Adjunct Professor at Norfolk State University.
Mrs. Ellis resides in Chesapeake, Virginia with her family. In her spare time, Claudine loves to travel, spend time with her family, and enjoys being an avid reader.

Made in the USA
Columbia, SC
16 November 2019